Praise for Magic Fishing Panties

"In the vein of Erma Bombeck, Dalferes presents her second collection of essays for gals of a 'certain age.' Like *I Was In Love With a Short Man Once*, gal readers get to stand in front of funhouse mirrors and laugh at the foibles of joining 'Club 50.' One word of warning: Gals, be sure you use the bathroom before you settle in to read. You know what I mean. *wink wink*"

—Betsy Ashton, Author of the Mad Max series, *Mad Max Unintended Consequences* and *Uncharted Territory*

"Funny, talented, and so relatable, Kimba Dalferes' new book is a must-read! She shares her hilarious adventures in a way that makes you wish you were there. The tattoo story is hysterical, and has one of my favorite lines, 'What's needed here is a spectacularly immature act.' I snort-laughed my wine out of my nose, but it was the most fun I'd had all day. GET THIS BOOK and settle in for an afternoon of unbridled belly laughs!"

—Vikki Claflin, Author, *Shake Rattle & Roll With It: Living & Laughing with Parkinson's*

"You're gonna wanna get into these pants – pronto! *Magic Fishing Panties* is Kim Dalferes at her finest: unapologetically funny and fresh, with stories so real you'll wish they happened to you, then sigh with relief that they didn't. Kim lives life laughing out loud with no regrets and oftentimes naked, surrounded by life-long friends who know how to use a kitty litter box. We are so very lucky she took the time to write it all down so we can go along for the ride, laughing all the way."

—Kathryn Mayer, Writer. Thinker. Doer. kathrynmayer.com

"*Magic Fishing Panties* is a candid and hilarious collection of stories about life in the middle years. Kimberly Dalferes is truly remarkable for her ability to take even the most mundane human moments and turn them into life lessons that are both funny and captivating in the way they remind us of the connectedness that we all share."

—Marquita Herald, Author, *The Resilient Living Collection*

"Take this book, a plate of cookies, and your favorite beverage to your easy chair and prepare to giggle and guffaw. Kim Dalferes, an award-winning writer of humorous short stories, is a superhero for those of us who need a jovial jester to ease our journey as we tumble down the back side of middle-age. Her costume usually includes fuzzy bunny slippers, an industrial-strength bra, and magic fishing panties. Her secret weapon to combat all the world's evil: Laugh until your gut hurts. Read her essays and laugh along with the rest of us."

—Elaine Ambrose, Author, *Midlife Cabernet*

"Getting older is made easier if you have a sense of humor. If you don't have one, you can borrow Kim Dalferes' who shares her adventures of becoming a woman of a certain age. You'll giggle, laugh and possibly snort out loud. Women at midlife will feel especially connected to the feelings and experiences Kim shares."

—Leslie Truex, Author, Speaker and Lifestyle Design Enthusiast, *leslietruex.com*

"Kimba Dalferes looks at midlife with a sense of humor and honesty. Covering everything from menopause to the empty nest on her blog, *The Middle-Aged Cheap Seats*, her new book *Magic Fishing Panties* will keep you laughing and nodding along with her as she explores the other side of fifty with her witty and wry voice."

—Sharon Greenthal, Founder, *Midlife Boulevard, midlifeboulevard.com*

"Kim Dalferes has done it again with another uproariously funny collection of tales chronicling the misadventures of her madcap life. She has mastered the art of storytelling by putting her unique spin on midlife mishaps guaranteed to tickle the funny bone. From tattoo parlors to gal pal confessions, this feisty book has it all and should be shared with your best friend. *Magic Fishing Panties* is witty, heartwarming and utterly addictive."

—Marcia Kester Doyle, Author, *Who Stole My Spandex?*

MAGIC FISHING PANTIES

More Tales from a Crazy Southern Irish Gal

Kimberly J. Dalferes

Booktrope Editions
Seattle WA 2015

Cover Design by Lizzie Russell

Edited by Anaik Alcasas

Proofread by Andie Gibson

Being that this is a work of creative nonfiction, the author would like to remind all readers that the stories contained within these pages are based upon her memory; which at 51 years old can, from time to time, have a few gaps. Some names and event descriptions have been changed to protect people's privacy. However, this book contains no story that does not have at least some basis in fact; events really did occur and what you are about to read is a reflection the author's best recollections. If you happen to remember some things differently, please give the author a call so you can compare notes.

Print ISBN 978-1-5137-0203-2

EPUB ISBN 978-1-5137-0245-2

Library of Congress Control Number: 2015911232

To my parents. Thank you for supporting all my foolishness. To be fair, your DNA is partly to blame.

For my gal pals. I love you all and would be lost without you.

Table of Contents

Introduction

THE CENTERS FOR Disease Control and Prevention (CDC) has concluded my average life expectancy is approximately seventy-nine years. When I read this it got me to thinking: According to the CDC, I hit middle-aged about a decade ago, right? If middle-aged is indeed the chronological mid-point of our lives, then I reached middle-aged status around thirty-nine.

Really?

What does middle-aged mean to most of us, aside from the numerical countdown? The term can be accompanied by a bit of a drab visual—old, boring, tired, frumpy, maybe even a bit sad. That's certainly not how I've thought of myself during this past decade.

Recently, I've noticed quite a bit of conjecture by the media regarding age, aging, anti-aging, youth, beauty, and wrinkles. Under headlines such as "Is Seventy the New Fifty?" everyone seems to be professing new benchmarks: forty is the new thirty or fifty is the new forty.

Here's an idea we should all try on for size:

Fifty is the new *fifty*. Period.

Yep, I've passed the Big 5-0. I'm DELIGHTED to be in my fifties! True, I would rather not be dealing with the injustices of menopause, but all decades bring challenges, obstacles, and joys:

> **My twenties** were a blur of attending and finishing college (a truly wonderful time in my life—GO NOLES!), landing my first real grown-up job, marriage, child birth—which brought to me a kindred spirit in my son, Jimmy—and the purchasing of my first home.

> **My thirties** featured the downfall of divorce, single parent-hood, a new wonderful independent life in DC—and with it a tremendous career boost.

> **My forties** offered a new marriage, seeing my son graduate from high school—and college (!)—and writing and publishing my first book, *I Was In Love With a Short Man Once.*

> **My fifties**—Bring it on!

One of the many facets of turning fifty is that fifty brings perspective. At fifty, you have arrived at the party. At fifty, you have become comfortable in your own skin. Don't get me wrong—I always have room for improvement. However, I find as I enter this sixth decade I've grown into my looks and my personality. I'm loud, I laugh at all the wrong parts of a movie, and I accept who I am. Fifty feels good, like a well-fitting red coat that looks perfect with the right pair of black boots.

As I'm now privileged to have reached the mid-century mark, there are a few life moments and realities that I've experienced and, I must admit, place me firmly in middle-aged territory. To borrow from the great comedian Jeff Foxworthy and his famous *You Might Be a Redneck If...* musings, below are my top ten observations.

You Might Be Middle Aged If...

1. You've become genuine friends with your kids and you actually ask them for advice.

2. Your hair is getting thinner everywhere except on your legs. (And where the hell did your eyebrows go?)

3. You've ever taken off your bra and it's as if an airbag has deployed.

4. You've ever walked into a room and can't for the life of you remember why.

5. You leave "readers" all over the house because the damn print has suddenly gotten *so* darn tiny.

6. You've ever taken to blaming the little people for stealing all the things you can't find (I sure wish they would return that Chico's gift card).

7. You've ever started a sentence with "Back when I was in school..."

8. You think Ryan Reynolds is hot and this might make you a cougar and you don't care.

9. You've ever been called a cougar. Hashtag idea: #EMBRACETHECOUGAR.

10. You've been best friends with someone for more than thirty-five years and she still thinks your dumb jokes are funny.

I believe I'm starting to enjoy the whole "age and experience over youth and exuberance" philosophy. The ol' gal staring back at me in the mirror each morning still has a bit of a twinkle in her eye, even if those eyes now have crow's feet. The view from the middle-aged cheap seats sure is interesting. What do I appreciate most about my perch in the cheap seats? My gal pals.

I've often been called a "guy's gal." This is usually, I think, meant as a compliment. There are some stereotypically masculine pursuits I do enjoy and which often lead me to rattling around in the boys' clubhouse. For example, I *love* football. I've followed the Dolphins since 1972 and as many of you know, I'm also a somewhat crazed Florida State fan. I can fish, tell jokes (yes, especially dirty ones), I love war movies, and have been known to go shot for shot with the gentlemen at the bar. I've yet to reach "broad" status, but I'm working on it. Call me a *broad-in-waiting*.

As I've gotten older, and a wee bit wiser (read: subject for debate), it's my gal pals who I dearly appreciate and cherish. Please don't get me wrong: I do like the boys, I truly do. Nevertheless, it's my gal pals who I've come to love with all my heart and soul. Here in Club Fifty, most of my best friends are girlfriends.

What's a travesty is the way female relationships are often por-trayed by the media. I personally boycott any show where a woman stabs another woman in the back, or throws a punch! I fear a whole generation of younger women watch this trash and believe this is an acceptable way for women to treat each other. WRONG!

There are so many things about gal pals that I value, it's difficult to narrow my rationale down to a few highlights. However, in no particular order, here are some of the reasons I love and need my gal pals every day:

You can go several months, or even years, without seeing each other and pick up right where you left off.

You can give an honest opinion. If you ask a gal pal "does this skirt make me look fat?" she's going to tell you the truth, but in the nicest way possible.

You can show your behind and it doesn't matter; it's even expected. I've gotten into some fabulous trouble with my gal pals. If you need evidence, the chapter called "Once Again, Naked In Public" is a good place to start.

You can talk too much, laugh too loud, and be too emotional. Gal pals don't judge, they hang in there with you and think it's funny when you laugh at all the wrong parts of a story.

You can be vulnerable when it comes to talking about relationships. I've divulged some of my deepest fears about family and men to my gal pals. Often, I'm not looking for an opinion. Sometimes, all you need is someone to listen and hold your hand. A gal pal understands this.

In addition to my true-life gal pals, I've also been building a list of my "virtual" gal pals—women I would love to meet and spend some time with over drinks and/or chocolate cake. Here's a sampling of my ultimate cocktail party invitees (and yes, some of these are posthumous, I never said this party wouldn't be happening in the next dimension):

Mae West. Did you know she was a playwright? Yep, her first play produced on Broadway was titled *Sex*. Authorities shut it down after one week and then she spent a week in jail for moral indecency. She was *way* ahead of her time.

Cleopatra. There is such a mystique surrounding this woman. She was married twice—fought a civil war against the first and poisoned the second. She had children by Julius Caesar and Mark Antony. This gal certainly ruled her world.

Katherine Hepburn. Ms. Hepburn is one of my all-time favorite actresses. I've seen a few interviews where she talks about the love of her life, Spencer Tracy. I would like to ask her if she was ever conflicted about being the "other woman."

Janet Reno. I had the good fortune to work at the Justice Department when Ms. Reno was Attorney General. Oh, if I could get fifteen minutes worth of off-the-record conversation.

Jennifer Lawrence. This young actress first earned my respect with her break-through performance in the movie *Winter's Bone* (if you missed it, *so* worth the rental). She truly won me over as I watched her fabulous reaction when Jack Nicholson crashed her Oscar night interview with George Stephanopoulos.

Margaret Thatcher. I never agreed with her politics. Nevertheless, she sure was confident in her convictions and shattered a big ol' British glass ceiling. Wouldn't it be a hoot to see a conversation between this Prime Minister and Attorney General Reno?

Cari Cucksey. Cari is the host of the HGTV show *Cash & Cari* which showcases her work as an estate sale coordinator. In addition to being an estate sale expert, she also owns the store *RePurpose*, a vintage shop where she sells her brilliant creations. Cari is definitely one of my women entrepreneur idols.

Gertrude Stein. Ms. Stein may be one of the most famous American expats who made Paris their home. If you've never read *The Autobiography of Alice B. Toklas* add it to your summer reading list.

Ann Joyce. Don't know who Ann Joyce is? She was my Nana. I would love beyond words to be able to talk to her as an adult and ask her questions such as: What was it like to be an immigrant to the U.S.? What was my great-grandmother like? And, please, what's the recipe for your legendary apple pie?

Tina Fey. Ms. Fey is one of my comedic heroes. When she coined the phrase "Bitch is the New Black" she locked up her place on my cocktail party top ten.

I've written this book, in part, for all my gal pals out there—both real and imagined. I hope we can meet up soon and get into all kinds of mischief together.

FAMILY REFLECTIONS

I'm saying this is the South. And we're proud of our crazy people. We don't hide them up in the attic. We bring 'em right down to the living room and show 'em off. See, no one in the South ever asks if you have crazy people in your family. They just ask what side they're on.

—Julia Sugarbaker, *Designing Women*

AH YES, FAMILY. Have you ever met anyone who didn't think their own clan was collectively off its rocker? Mine is quite a mixed bag: Irish, Southern, extended, blended, multi-generational—you name it and we're probably somehow affiliated.

While sitting up here in the middle-aged cheap seats I've often looked in the rearview mirror and thanked the universe for a family that is uniquely mine. I have wonderful memories of all four grandparents. Each was a gift to me and all were exceptional individuals. My parents helped shape who I am. I blame my behavior on their DNA all the time. I'm also forever indebted to my little brother, Scotty, whose shenanigans and hell-raising allowed me to fly under the radar for many years. Thanks for the cover Bro; I owe you one.

A few years ago I went on an ancestry discovery binge and mapped out both sides of my family, at times being able to go back as far as the 1400s! I discovered a possible lineage to Princess Margaret Tudor, sister to King Henry the VIII (on my mama's side). As fascinating as the bloodlines can be, I find it's the family stories that are so much more interesting than a possible connection to Mayflower descendants (Edmund Masterson, a thirteenth great grandfather). I've discovered my grandfather was the creator of a newsletter called *The Snotty Sneeze,* I have an uncle who lost a leg in World War I, and my other grandfather liked to attend cockfights (under the guise of attending union meetings on Saturday afternoons). These are the stories I wish someone had written down.

What follows are a few tales about the members of my tribe. I love each and every one of them, quirks and all.

Peas Behind the Washer

HAVE YOU EVER LOVED an inanimate object? Rationally, we should love people, and special moments, and extraordinary memories, not material goods, right? Wouldn't it be futile to love possessions that don't seem to have capacity to love us back? Not always. Sometimes we are offered objects that provide powerful sources of love, joy, and warmth. I've had the good fortune to have loved such an object. I loved my grandparents' house. That house truly had a soul and loved and protected our family in very special ways.

When I was young, I believed their house was an enchanted palace. It was crafted in the traditional Spanish architecture of South Florida, with white stucco walls and black shutters and an arched, heavy wooden front door. However, as a child, I had no awareness of the architectural style of the home. I only thought of the house on Omar Road as the safest place on earth.

This home was where my mom and her brothers and sister grew up. We would listen intently during family gatherings as stories of their childhood were passed along to all the kids, including myself, little brother Scotty, and my bevy of first cousins. Beloved stories were often repeated each year, as is the way of oral histories. There was the time my sleep-walking Uncle Sammy came running down the stairs mid-nightmare and scared the hell out of my mom who had just returned from seeing *Psycho* at the movies. There were frequent descriptions of how my Aunt Terry would aggravate my mom at the dinner table by pinching the tops of her feet with her toes. So many stories of shared bedrooms, sibling pranks, and beloved all-night gabfests.

I also have my own recollections of time spent in my grandparents' house. I remember in great detail much of its interior, such as the upright piano that greeted everyone who walked through the front door. There was a wonderful black rotary phone perched on a small table at the top of the stairs. The only bathroom in the house was encased in shiny pink tiles. The dining room floor had a permanent and noticeable slant and the china cabinet contents would tinkle against each other and sound the alarm to slow down if you rushed by too fast. Within the home's walls, I learned to cook and sew and make proper hot tea.

The enchantments of this house were not limited to its contents. The surrounding yard also reflected the talents of a gifted Southern woman. I often fondly recall my Gramma's prized avocado tree, which each year produced a bounty of football-sized green beauties. There was a melaleuca tree with bark that shredded off in layers like thick, spongy paper. We kids—the hellions we were—often got into trouble for playfully stripping away that tree trunk. In our defense, it was quite irresistible; like the popping of bubble wrap.

The holidays, especially Thanksgiving, were almost always celebrated at my grandparents' house. All the heathens—as my Grumps so fondly referred to his grandchildren—would voice feeble protests about being relegated to the "kiddie table" on the back porch. Weak rationales were offered as to there not being enough room for the entire family to congregate around the dining room table. The truth was, we loved our back porch banishment. Back in that small little room we were unfettered by any pretense of good holiday table manners or proper etiquette. There was something about the gathering of cousins which often made us lose all semblance of self-control. The grownups frequently needed a break from us.

Dinner always began with the best of intentions. The saying of grace was a respected ritual. Even sequestered on the back porch we could clearly hear Grumps bless the meal and offer his favorite prayer tagline: *and please make Scotty a good boy.* Warnings always followed: BEHAVE. Cousin John usually smiled slyly as the porch door swung shut behind Gramma.

The cousins would maintain the façade of composure for, at the most, fifteen minutes. Inevitably, each year it would start with a random piece of food, perhaps a chunk of turkey, being dunked into someone's milk. Peas would begin to be placed up noses, only to be dislodged by a squirt of our turkey-laden beverages. Mashed potatoes would follow, being flung past a ducking cousin Brian, to hit and fall behind the washing machine with a bit of a dull thud.

Our squeals of delight were not lost on the adults assembled in the not-so-far-away dining room. They knew, they had to have known, what we were up to. We would get away with our shenanigans for a short while, but our uncle's booming "Ya'll better clean that up!" would most often bring us back to our senses.

As the years passed, our sanctuary eventually became too much for Gramma to handle on her own. She sold our beloved safe haven and moved to Jacksonville to live with her sister in 1986, ten years after my Grumps had departed this world. Right before her move we were back at the house helping with the packing, sorting, and culling of treasured keepsakes. The house looked different as seen through my adult eyes, and yet there were aspects that remained unchanged. It seemed smaller, but the dining room floor still slanted and the tiles in the bathroom were still pink and the piano was still anchored against the wall near the front door.

I walked through the rooms littered with packing boxes and soon found myself on that back porch. The washing machine had been pulled away from the wall and there, stacked against the wood slats that had never seen daylight, was what looked to be the remnants of an archeological dig. Years of food fights were immortalized by layers of fossilized food. It looked like an intricate cross-cut section of a deep gravel pit. I smiled broadly as memories of the glorious

mess we made each year danced in my head, and I quietly acknowl-
edged my gratitude for a house that had protected and preserved
our antics in the hidden spaces behind the washer.

Gramma and Grumps are both in heaven now; she joined him
there in 1999. When I think of them, I almost always picture them
together in the house on Omar Road. Do you think the heavenly
version of the home where they reside includes a back porch with
a washing machine that conceals the remnants of Thanksgivings
past? I hope so, I truly do.

*   *   *

*This essay earned honorable mention as part of the 2014 Virginia Writers
Club (VWC) Summer Shorts Contest. It will be included in the 2014 VWC
Anthology to be published early 2015.*

Wide Calves

IN GENERAL, I'M QUITE FOND of the way we talk in the South. I grew up with terms such as dressing (not stuffing), supper (not dinner), and soda (not pop). However, having lived in Northern Virginia (NOVA) for the past nineteen years, I've lost most of my Southern drawl, except when I'm tired or drinking tequila. If I'm tired AND drinking I often sound like Dolly Parton. You would think NOVA inhabitants would exhibit the telltale Southern twang, but we seem to have morphed into one of those multi-cultural geographic regions where accents are ambiguous or non-existent. Nonetheless, when it comes to talking—which I do quite often—I've not lost my ability to—on occasion, accent or not—put my foot in my mouth. Is this a Southern thing or a Kimba thing? Hmmm...

On both sides of my family we have a tendency to speak first, ask questions later. Opinions flow as rapidly as the Mississippi river. One is never wrong, one's opponent is merely misinformed, so let us explain things properly. My Uncle Tommy is legendary for arguing about anything, anywhere, taking the opposite viewpoint solely to get a rise out of ya. This propensity to debate non-stop drives his sisters bat-crap crazy. The cousins, especially during the holidays, egg him on just to watch our moms go off the rails a bit. Yep, we're a warped bunch, for sure. We are also quite notorious for butchering the English language.

I possess a rich personal history of misspoken moments. My patron saint should be the great Yogi Berra, who uttered such beauties as:

A nickel ain't worth a dime anymore.

If you come to a fork in the road, take it.

And a personal favorite, since I hail from the sunshine state:

It ain't the heat, it's the humility.

One particular misspoken humdinger forever ingrained in my memory bubbles up each time I'm at the beach and I spy a Portuguese man-of-war. If you've never seen a man-of-war please know you really shouldn't mess with them. Along Florida's shores they come in with the tide and often become stranded on the beach. They dot the sand like misshapen plastic bubbles, with long colorful ribbons cascading around them. It's those ribbons you have to be on the lookout for: stepping on the tendrils of a man-of-war, which are quite poisonous, can be exceptionally painful.

One sunny day back in my high school heydays, while walking along the beach with a large group of teenage friends, we came upon several man-of-wars that had washed ashore together. I remember loudly declaring,

"Look out for the testicles on that one!"

High school kids, even your best friends, are not going to let you live that one down for a very, very long time.

I also recall an occasion, much later in life, when I was once again out with friends, this time in a more adult environment. Yeah, OK, we were out drinking. We were attending a conference in Cincinnati and had decided to venture out to experience the local night life. We discovered a wonderful sports bar—sure wish I could remember the name of the place—serving cheap beer and hot wings where we could watch football on the various televisions, shoot pool, and bang on the tables during a resounding rendition of *Tainted Love*. I usually take great pride in being able to hang with the boys when it comes to handling my liquor. However, on this particular evening I was drinking quite a bit; we all were. One of the guys got so drunk he proposed to the waitress and bought her flowers. To this day we have no idea where he found a bouquet of daisies at midnight in a downtown sports bar. As sometimes happens, I too over-indulged and "Jezebel," my alter ego, emerged.

Late into the evening, in her somewhat sodden stupor, Jezebel spied a poor soul across the bar sporting a white Miami sweatshirt. Jezebel, forever the Florida State fan, went straight to it; she truly couldn't help herself.

"Hey... hey!" Jezebel exclaimed.

No response.

"Hey you, yeah, you in the Miami sweatshirt!"

The puzzled guy slowly looked our way with a quizzical *you talking to me?* look on his face.

"Yeah, you! We kicked your Hurricane ass in football!"

Snickering ensued all around.

"Whatcha all laughing at?!" declared Jezebel indignantly. "We did! The Noles kicked their ass this year! GO NOLES!"

My buddy Randy walked around the table, put his arm around me, and with a big ol' grin on his face asked me/Jezebel in his low, slow Missouri drawl,

"Darlin' do you think he might be from, oh I don't know, Miami... of Ohio?"

"Huh? Oh. Ooohhhh..." It sometimes takes a moment for Jez to catch on.

"Hey, Miami guy, sorry! No hard feelings!"

To his credit, Mr. Miami Sweatshirt Fella simply chuckled and walked away. Jez should have bought him a drink.

Years later my buddies still check in with me during the FSU/ Miami football game, just to make sure I'm tuned-in. Jerk faces.

It appears I've passed along the malapropism gene to my off-spring, Jimmy. For example, when he was in high school he was selected to travel and tour Europe one summer with the Virginia honor band. As the band parents corralled their kids at the airport, waiting to send them off through security, the conversation turned to the lower drinking age in Europe and who was going to be allowed to drink alcohol. My son interjected with,

"While we're in Italy, I'm going to try one of those Roman Cokes."

"A what?" I asked.

"You know, a Roman Coke. I've seen you order those before. What's in one?"

"Honey, do you mean a *rum and coke*?"

"Huh? Oh yeah, of course," he replied with a laugh and a bit of a blush.

Love that kid. Being that he's now graduated from college and attending graduate school, I can guarantee he possesses up close and personal knowledge of the ingredients for a rum and coke.

Regarding the family tribe, both my gaffes and the blunders of my son, as funny as they may be, reside as mere honorable mentions in the family blooper hall of fame. The reigning champ is my mom. In the family chronicles of the finest example of using a word out of context, it's difficult to believe anyone will ever top the beauty Mom let loose a couple of Thanksgivings ago. What makes this particularly ironic is that my mom, unlike her daughter and her grandson, is not a loud mouth. She is downright soft-spoken compared to the rest of our clan of opinionated extroverts. She does not regale in notoriety.

When my grandmother moved on, our family lost its central location for gatherings. We've had to adjust by rotating the location for holiday celebrations among the family members. On the occasions when we've celebrated Thanksgiving at my Aunt Terry's house in Atlanta, we've developed a wonderful post-Thanksgiving ritual: shoe shopping.

Atlanta and its suburbs are quite the shoe shopping mecca. For a girl like me who has sported size elevens since I was in the eighth grade, discovering an enclave of stores carrying big-girl shoes at great prices is right up there with the creation of penicillin, Spanx, and Dove chocolate. Each trip to Atlanta I plan for at least one additional suitcase just to bring back my shoe finds.

On this one particular post-Thanksgiving shoe shopping expedition we were a girls-only bunch. Boys don't get wound up over shoes the way we gals do. Boys get excited over pizza toppings and sandwich fixins. We girls have our stilettos. Seems like a fair trade.

Mom, Aunt Terry and my two cousins Amy and Gina entered the first store with me and we fanned out across the aisles. This store's no-frills approach heightened my senses as I perceived many bargains lurking in the stacks and along the crowded walls. I would not be disappointed. In the expansive size eleven section toward the back I discovered heels, clogs, flats, and boots. Sandals and flip flops from the summer season were intermixed with sling-backs and sensible close-toed pumps. These shoes looked like the shoes all the other girls get to wear, not the size eleven construction site work boots or dominatrix style heels most stores seem to believe a size eleven girl wants to sport.

I gathered up my top five choices and teetered over to where Mom, aunt, and the cousins were waiting for me near some chairs. This was my favorite part: I would model my choices like a New York runway model. First up was a pair of practical black pumps. As I sauntered past, Mom and Terry gave a thumbs up, the cousins were a split decision. A sales clerk helped seal the deal when she mentioned these pumps happened to be marked down an additional thirty percent AND they were also available, in my size, in red and blue. Sold!

Next came an awesome pair of brown leather boots for less than $100! I had my heart set on these boots, but, when I put them on, they didn't seem to fit right. The leather was way too big up around the top.

The same sales clerk who had been watching over us noticed my hesitation.

"Those are the wrong boots for you dear. They're for wide calves."

Mom, without missing a beat, looked at the sales clerk and said, "But, she *is* white."

Have I mentioned the sales clerk was African-American? No? Well, yeah.

The sales clerk looked at my mom incredulously. One of those *did you really just say that?!* moments. She opened her mouth, hesitated, closed it, and then slowly walked away.

"Mom! Are you nuts?!"

"Why? What did I do? She's the one who said you have white calves."

My cousins started snickering…uncontrollably. Aunt Terry leaned in and said softly,

"She didn't say the boots were for *white* calves, she said the boots were for *wide* calves."

"What? Oh…I see. Well, damn."

We had to leave the store…quickly. I couldn't bring myself to make eye contact with the sales clerk, or any of the staff, as we hurriedly made our way through the front door and out into the parking lot. Once inside the car we pretty much lost all control as my mom desperately tried to defend her position.

"You know, it was an honest mistake, could have happened to anyone."

Nope, not anyone, just the members of my family. This story gets retold each Thanksgiving and each year becomes a little more exaggerated. I think in the last rendition we caused a riot and had to be bailed out of jail. Poor Mom, stuck in a family of tall-tale tellers. Mom is hoping for another gaffe soon. Let someone else claim the coveted hall of fame top honors trophy. No worries Mom, in this family, I'm certain someone will eventually topple you.

Easter Egg Roll

I'VE ALWAYS WANTED to be a DC insider. Not the see-and-be-seen kind of insider, not the big-money-socialite-as-featured-in-*The-Washington-Post* insider—those are circles which I'll never reach on my household budget. I instead aspire to be an in-the-know DC insider. The type of person who can identify all the best tourist attractions, not only the usual monuments such as the Jefferson, Lincoln, and Washington, but also the off-the-beaten-path types of places. For example, the best park to take your kids to run around? The Teddy Roosevelt National Park. Where can you find a Darth Vader gargoyle? The National Cathedral. The very best place for blueberry pancakes? Eastern Market.

I've been honing my DC insider skills for the past two decades. One must spend quite a bit of quality time taking in the sights of our nation's capital in order to develop a solid working inventory of all things touristy. I've got the basics down cold: how to use the metro, book a tour of the Capitol, or find discount tickets for places that charge admission—such as the Newseum and the International Spy Museum—are all skills I have mastered. The Smithsonian museums in particular are a treasure trove of insider tidbits. A convenient indoor McDonalds can be found at Air and Space. The National Gallery of Art has a tasty gelato bar on its sub-ground level. In the summer a lovely place to take a break from the heat is the National Navy Memorial which showcases a fun fountain and lots of places to sit.

I've also tackled the must-do-at-least-once list. I've attended many parades, including the Chinese New Year Celebration in Chinatown and the St. Patrick's Day Parade. I've attended Mass at the National Cathedral on Christmas Eve, seen shows at the Kennedy Center (some for free!), watched the fireworks on the Mall on the Fourth of July, and visited the pandas at the National Zoo. Almost every experience was wonderful, glad to have done it at least once. *Almost* every experience.

The White House Easter Egg Roll is a tradition spanning all the way back to the mid-1800s. The event, which occurs the Monday following Easter, originally started on the grounds of the U.S. Capitol. In 1877, when members of Congress were working to balance budgets and cut corners (sound familiar?), they reduced funding for landscaping and grounds upkeep. In order to prevent damage and wear and tear, they passed a law forbidding the Capitol grounds to be used as a "children's playground." This included the annual Easter Egg Roll. The story goes that in 1878 President Hayes offered up the South Lawn at the White House to continue the tradition— take *that* Congress! And so it has been ever since, only to be canceled by complications such as bad weather and World Wars I and II.

When I moved to the DC area in the summer of 1995, taking my son to the White House Easter Egg Roll was high on my list of must-do events. Ironically, I don't like eggs, haven't been willing to eat them my whole life; truly nasty. Gratefully, the White House Easter Egg Roll doesn't require you to consume eggs, only that your child roll a hard-boiled egg across the lawn. By 1997, when my son was six, I was ready to get us on the lawn. Time was short: the age range for attending was three through six, so this was our final shot. Attending this event was so high on my must-do list I even implored my mom to come up from Florida for the festivities. She happily obliged. She would do anything for her grandson.

In 1997—the pre-Internet, pre-cell phone, pre-almost-all-technology days—the White House Easter Egg Roll organizers were in the infancy of effective crowd control. They had at least moved to timed-tickets, with efforts to limit the number of children and families moving through the gates and across the expansive lawns each hour. It should be noted this was also pre-9/11: strollers, large diaper bags, and backpacks all were allowed. I'm sure these days the screening process is a bit more rigorous. There is now a lottery for tickets, with 300,000 applying in 2014 for 30,000 tickets (though still free of charge for those lucky lottery winners). To think I once complained about standing in line for a coveted entrance permit.

On a beautiful, breezy April morning, with not a cloud in the sky, Jimmy, Mom and I moved through the South Lawn check point at our assigned time and shuffled out into the sea of little people gleefully running across the landscape. It was a symphony of over-stimulation. Booths were set up to offer tchotchkes such as coloring books, pencils, balloons as well as literature on topics ranging from breastfeeding to the importance of pre-K education. Costumed characters mingled among the children. SpongeBob SquarePants was a particularly popular fella for both photo-eager parents as well as shrieking little ones. Over to the right was "Roll Down Mountain" where children could tumble downhill and, along the way, grind in grass stains and ruin the cute outfits their parents had stressed over. We merged into the 360-degree panoramic vision of pastels and ribbons. Jimmy was a bit overwhelmed. As he held tightly to his G-Ma's hand, I sought the Holy Grail of the event: the Easter Egg Roll.

The line (of course there was a line) snaked back and forth across a flat area of the lawn. I thought it wise to take care of this particularly important target so as to not miss out within our allotted time frame. Surprisingly, the line for the roll moved quickly and as the three of us reached the front, a sweet young woman informed us only one adult would be able to move into the egg rolling area with our child.

In response, someone I refer to as *That Girl* proceeded to take over. Now, I'm not proud of *That Girl*. *That Girl* manifests in those times in my life when I don't think before I speak. *That Girl* is always on a mission. *That Girl* has an agenda and she doesn't care at all who gets caught up in *That Girl's* wake.

"What?! Oh I don't think so. My mom here came all the way from Florida to see her grandson roll an egg across the White House lawn, and she's going to see her grandson roll that egg right now. Come on, Mom."

With that I took Jimmy's hand and moved onward into the egg rolling area. Mom looked at the young woman—I'm sure she was an intern who was merely trying to keep some semblance of order in a chaotic situation—and gave her a sheepish shrug and moved forward with us. As we moved into the staging area for the roll, I definitely heard someone in the line behind us utter:

"Well, if they get to have two adults go with their kid, then why can't I do it?!"

That Girl had struck again. I'm genuinely sorry about this. I swear I don't let her out nearly as often as I used to.

In the staging area they lined up four children and armed them with large plastic spoons, the kind used for stirring soups or serving chili. There on the ground in front of each of them was a colorful hard-boiled egg. As a whistle blew, the startled kids were cheered on to reach down and *roll* the eggs across the small area to the finish line. The rolling part quickly devolved into what could be more accurately described as modified croquet, where the kids sort of smashed at the egg to propel it forward. One little guy gave up, scooped the egg up into his hands, and hurled it across the finish line. I must say, the kid had a pretty good arm.

The little exercise took all of twenty seconds and there at the other side of the finish line, collecting the spoons, was a generous soul who handed each of the participants a beautiful painted wooden egg, etched with the year of the roll and a pretty little logo. Each parent quickly took possession of the keepsake and stored it away for safekeeping.

We were now free to roam the event without an agenda. Seeing the President and First Lady would have been a treat. Alas, I overheard rumors there had been a sighting earlier in the morning—drat.

The storytelling tent would be offering another reading in thirty minute and every parent knows that camping out at story time is code for giving mom and dad a break. However, Jimmy spied a row of booths exhibiting age-appropriate educational toys and begged us to go investigate. But, *of course*. After all, this was his day to have fun. What could go wrong?

There are some moments in life so significant, years later you'll continue to instantly recall in full slow-motion detail how things went down. What transpired next remains forever ingrained in my memory, and is my go-to thought whenever I hear the words: "What could possibly go wrong?"

The three of us started to make our way toward the display booths as Jimmy's little hand slipped from mine and he eagerly moved out a short distance ahead of us. The crowd was thick but I kept my eyes on him as I chatted with Mom about God knows what. Perhaps we were admiring our newly acquired wooden egg. I could see Jimmy making a beeline for a colorful display: a table which had propped upon it a large American flag, made out of red, white, and blue plastic and interlocking pieces and mounted onto a heavy wooden frame. Not exactly Lego bricks, but created along the same lines.

At the exact moment Jimmy reached the display, a large gust of April wind rushed across the area and hit the back side of the booth. The flag fixture mounted onto the large wooden frame, backed with plywood and positioned on top of the table, was anchored to—nothing! The gust of wind caught the frame at just the right angle and the whole display came toppling over, falling directly onto Jimmy.

I do not recall what I said. Guttural sounds came up and out of me that I'm certain were channeled from some deep, ancient place reserved for moms when their offspring are in danger. I do recollect that after issuing a collective gasp, the crowd parted almost instantaneously as I swooped in, removing the display from atop of my son with one quick movement. I've heard urban legends about mothers being able to lift cars when their children are trapped beneath. I now believe those myths to be fully factual. There I sat on the ground, holding Jimmy in my lap and frantically checking him for broken bones, missing teeth, or any signs of blood.

"Oh, my gosh, is your son OK?!" called out the booth attendees as they frantically approached us on the other side of their display.

I ignored them. I wasn't letting any of these careless people within a mile of Jimmy.

"Jimmy, Jimmy, are you OK? Does anything hurt?"

To this day I remember Jimmy didn't say a word. He simply looked up at me and nodded his head up and down.

"Jimmy, honey, tell Mom if anything hurts."

"I'm OK," he replied. However, he didn't try to get up off the ground and out of my lap—not a typical reaction for a six-year-old boy. Startled, scared, or seriously hurt, I couldn't tell.

My mom, the ever-present voice of reason, tapped me gently on the shoulder and softly said,

"Kim, there are some paramedics here who want to look at Jimmy. You need to let them examine him."

It was at this moment I began to regain some semblance of the fact that Jimmy and I were sitting in the middle of a nice little developing scene. We were encircled by a small crowd that was pushing in to see what all the hubbub was about.

From behind Mom emerged a nice young man in navy pants and white pocketed shirt with some sort of colorful patch on the upper arms of each sleeve.

"Ma'am? Hi. We would like to walk you and your son over to our first aid tent. Can your son walk?"

"Yes, yes, I think so," I replied.

Jimmy stood up first and then I slowly got myself into a prone position. My legs were wobbly and the crowd was causing me to feel disoriented. There was, in all probability, a fair to large amount of adrenaline coursing through my body. By divine grace I did not faint.

As we walked toward the first aid tent, the paramedics made small talk with Jimmy.

"How old are you? ... Wow, only six? I would've thought you were a lot older."

"What grade are you in?"

"What school do you go to? What's your teacher's name?"

The paramedic was assessing Jimmy for signs of trauma. Jimmy's answers were clear and responsive. God love that kid, never met a stranger. Good thing they weren't asking me many questions; I probably would have thrown up.

When we reached the tent they checked Jimmy more thoroughly, looking for scrapes, bruises, or any sign of a broken bone. And then, there it was, a small trickle of blood on the top of his head. The paramedic found a small gash buried on Jimmy's scalp. The injury was not very big or deep, but they noted we should watch Jimmy for signs of a concussion and consider taking him to an emergency room or urgent care center.

"I can't tell you how sorry we are about this happening," came a voice from behind me, interrupting my conversation with the first aid tent staff. I turned to find one of the booth attendees who must have followed us as we traversed across the lawn.

"Can we give your son a present?" they feebly asked. "We feel so bad about this."

In her outstretched hands was a motorized car made from the same interlocking plastic pieces that had comprised the flag display.

"Sure!" responded Jimmy as he held out his hands to accept the toy.

I glared at the woman. Mom laid a hand on my arm and responded, "Thank you. We know it was an accident."

"We are so, so, sorry." Turning to Jimmy, she added, "Is there anything else we can get for you?"

Regaining some of my composure, I said aloud,

"Jimmy, tell her you want to meet Hillary."

This got a bit of a laugh from those in the tent and a sigh of relief from Mom. Her daughter was getting her proverbial sh*t back together.

We did watch Jimmy for signs of concussion for the remainder of the day. Keeping him awake in the taxi on the way back to the metro was a challenge. In the end, as these stories often turn out, he was just fine. That motorized car sat in a coveted space on his toy shelf for many years. Over time we've sadly lost track of it.

We do still have that wooden egg. Each Easter I fetch it out of the decorations bin and place it front and center on the fireplace mantel. It always reminds me of a few life lessons:

—don't be *That Girl*,

—accidents happen,

—and a mother's love will move mountains, or an American flag.

No Man's Land

MORE THAN A DECADE AGO, in the summer of 2003, the Transportation Security Administration (TSA) was, to be frank, working its proverbial sh*t out. It had been little more than eighteen months since 9/11 and in that short time the fledgling TSA had accomplished some remarkable things. It's mind-boggling to comprehend how quickly U.S. transportation systems evolved in order to protect our safety and ensure safe passage. However, there were, in the beginning, a few kinks in the system.

The family vacation in the summer of '03 was a weeklong excursion down to Key West. If you've never been to the Keys, you must go, but not in August. Well, unless you like saunas. If you like saunas, go in August.

Dad and stepmom Mary rented a large Key West house for the week and the family all made plans to converge from our various abodes across the U.S. Husband Greg, Jimmy and I, because we reside on the East Coast, had one of the easiest flights since we could fly direct out of DC. Or, at least that's what we thought.

This trip began with none of the usual last-minute theatrics. We managed to be fully packed the night before. Our handy-dandy checklist was all taken care of: paper held, dog squared away at the kennel, bathing suits and sunscreen tucked into the suitcases.

Greg, for once, was not only on time the next morning, but actually managed to get us out of the house ahead of schedule. I should have known the fates were up to something.

Dulles International Airport is a quagmire of modern design. After passing through the main terminal security checkpoints, you must queue into people movers that ferry you across the tarmac over to the various gates. In the years since 2003 the folks who manage Dulles have improved the system somewhat, but it remains an odd navigation path to reach your gate of departure. You must factor in an additional thirty to sixty minutes of time at the airport, because you never know what types of delays you might encounter within the terminal. I have friends in the DC area who flat out refuse to fly out of Dulles for no reason other than it's a total crap shoot as to whether you will make it to your gate in time for boarding.

On this particular trip, which had begun so swimmingly, we believed the luck of the travel god to be with us. We sailed through security at the main terminal, rode comfortably and without incident over to our satellite terminal via the people mover, and found ourselves with enough time to sit for a bit at one of the fast food restaurants and grab coffee, bagels, donuts, and OJ. There are few times during my travels with the Hubs and the Kiddo that I've not experienced the rush of running full sprint, bags rolling and teetering precariously behind us, as we barely make it to the gate. Hubs seems to relish the feel-the-burn charge of sprinting down the carpeted corridor, to breathlessly hand his boarding pass to a stoic flight attendant mere seconds before the gate door closes. Me…not so much. For me, having enough time to get coffee and make a final bathroom stop before boarding had the makings of a blessed day. Until…

Group three was called to board the plane and we queued up with our boarding passes in hand, Greg first, then Jimmy, followed by *moi*. Greg passed through, the beep sound from the scanning device confirming his boarding pass had been accepted. Without looking back, he headed down the jetway. Jimmy went next and then, just as I handed over my ticket and the reassuring beep from the scanner was heard, Jimmy wheeled around and pronounced:

"Mom! I left my jacket on the table in front of Burger King."

This was not some clothing heirloom. This was a worn, cotton, dark blue Old Navy zip-up hoodie. At the most it would have cost $15 to replace. Nevertheless, it was Jimmy's favorite jacket and if you comprehend anything about tweens, it's that their mood can go from gleeful to sullen in .03 seconds based on nothing more than having lost their cheap-ass jacket that would be too small for them in a month anyway. I immediately assessed I did not want to risk a three-hour flight with said surliness.

Turning back around to the flight attendant, I asked:

"Oh, do we have time for my son to go back and retrieve his jacket? He left it right over there outside of Burger King."

As I pointed back over her shoulder, you could see the navy blue jacket still lying across the top of the round, white table in the center of the wide area in front of Burger King.

"Oh, I think we have time," answered the attendant as she smiled sweetly at Jimmy. As we moved back off the jetway and out of the way of the other passengers, she noted, "Go ahead and go get your jacket and then come back here to me."

Jimmy went running over toward the table as I mouthed the words "Thank you" to the attendant who had that all-knowing *I'm a parent of a tween, too* look about her.

As Jimmy came sprinting back toward us, jacket in hand, another flight attendant, a smallish man with stern facial features and glasses that sat low across the bridge of his nose, walked over to our flight attendant—let's call her Maggie—and asked in an exasperated tone:

"What are you doing?"

Without looking up or over at him, Maggie kept right on moving the tickets through the scanner, beeping the passengers along. She tersely responded:

"What? I'm not doing anything but working. What are *you* doing?"

This seemed to set off—let's call him Oscar—Oscar in a way that reeked of this was going to get ugly.

"Well, you know they can't get on the plane now, right? They've crossed back out and off of the jetway."

I have no idea if this was the official security policy and proto-col of 2003. Apparently the rules at that time were kind of being interpreted as need be and necessary. It appeared the jetway was a bit of a no man's land: one flight attendant owned you when you entered the gangplank, an awaiting attendant on the plane owned you as soon as you stepped over the threshold and onto the plane. The space in between was a wasteland area where no one was technically responsible for you. It makes sense that the jetway was designed, is still designed, to funnel you in one direction: onto the plane. We had, it would seem, violated the temporal order of the universe by going backwards instead of forward.

"Oh, give me a break," replied Maggie. "The kid went to go get his jacket." As if on cue Jimmy came running back up to us at this precise moment. "I could see him the whole time."

"Well, I don't care," replied Oscar. "I'm calling security," he exclaimed as he wheeled around in a huff and stalked over to the gate check-in counter.

"This is ridiculous. I need to finish the check in and get everyone onboard," Maggie noted loudly enough for Oscar, who now had a phone to his ear, to hear from his perch back behind the counter.

"I'm sorry, could you and your son please wait over here to the side until we get this straightened out?" Maggie asked of me as I was trying to take in exactly what was happening here.

"Of course, sure," I replied as Jimmy and I moved over to a row of seats in the waiting area to the right, in order to let the other passengers board the plane.

"I'm sorry, Mom," said my red-faced son. "Why are we in trouble?"

"Honey, we're not in trouble. We just need to wait until every-one else goes through boarding and then we'll be able to get on the plane, too." This was at least my hope.

Maggie quickly finished the boarding process for groups four and five, as all the while Jimmy and I stood hovering over to the side. As she flagged through the last person, she paced purposefully over to Oscar who was still standing behind the counter.

"Look, I need to get these two onto the plane."

"Not until security gets here," replied Oscar.

"What?! This is ridiculous! You actually called security?!"

Maggie made no attempt to hide her exasperation, and being that we were a mere few feet away we were in full view of what was transpiring.

"Yep, that's protocol, the protocol *you* breached. I suggest you inform the crew that we have a delay if you want those two to make the flight."

This was beginning to piss *me* off. *Those two*? What the hell? This jerk face was going to make us miss our flight over a bat-crap crazy idea that some sort of invisible barrier had been penetrated. I reared up, but just as my mouth opened to chime in, Jimmy touched my arm, whispering to me,

"Mom, don't do it. Let them work this out. You'll only make it worse."

I hate it when the kid is right.

Unbeknownst to us, there was a little bit of a hubbub occurring on the plane as well. Greg had turned around in the aisle to help lift our luggage into the overhead bins, when he realized we were not immediately behind him. He moved into his seat, but as he quickly ascertained we were not on the plane, he waved over a flight attendant to ask:

"My wife and son were right behind me, but they don't seem to have gotten on the plane. Do you know if they are still at the gate?"

"Hmm, I'm not sure, sir. Let me check."

The attendant returned a few minutes later and answered,

"There's been a slight delay in the boarding process. I'm sure everyone will be onboard shortly."

Oh, but we weren't. It took security another thirty minutes to arrive at the gate. Jimmy and I had started to seriously sweat out our predicament. I kept reassuring Jimmy, and myself, that as long as the plane remained at the gate, we would be fine. All the while, Maggie and Oscar continued their arguing, taking their bickering just out of earshot. However, their body language gave it all away: they both had their backs up.

Two muscular men in uniform finally arrived, walking past us and over to Maggie and Oscar where they began to question the attendants. We were unable to hear everything that transpired, but I definitely heard Maggie utter the word "bonehead" and Oscar throw out "improper procedure."

Back on the plane, Greg had taken note that the only two remaining empty seats were those next to him on his row. The problem must be with his wife and son. Right when he was about to get up and ask to also leave the plane, the pilot came on with this announcement:

"Ladies and gentlemen, I apologize for this brief delay. It appears that two of our passengers have experienced some sort of problem with security. I'm sure we will be leaving soon."

Oh, geez, thought Greg, *Now what has she done?* Did he get off the plane? Oh, hell no. He wasn't going to miss out on Key West because his nutso wife had gone and pissed someone off—again. Well, his staying on the plane was kind of a blessing. The last thing we needed was for the Hubs to be in the middle of all the craziness.

After what seemed to be an eternity, the security guys nodded to the attendants and made their way over to where Jimmy and I had been maintaining our sentry positions. We had been standing next to the row of waiting area seats adjacent to the gate door the whole time, with the keen belief that as long as the door remained miraculously open, we still had a shot at getting on the plane.

"Hello, what's your name?" the taller of the two officers asked my son.

"Jimmy Budnick, sir." (The *sir* was a nice touch, don't you think?)

"Well, Jimmy, if we can take a quick look at your jacket and in your backpack, we'll be able to let you and your mom get on your plane."

"Sure!" Jimmy responded, as if to convey: Hey, I'm a really good kid. Please don't shoot me.

The other officer smiled over at me as the first quickly, and I mean like a millisecond's worth of time, rummaged through Jimmy's pack, gave his jacket a brief squeeze, and then turned to the attendants and said quite officially,

"They are cleared to go."

Yes, the free world had just been saved for all mankind.

As Jimmy and I crossed back onto the jetway, and the door shut behind us, I distinctly heard Maggie call to Oscar: "You, are a douche."

No truer words have ever been spoken.

Unfortunately, we were not quite done. As we crossed over the threshold onto the plane, I realized the inside of the plane went completely silent. All eyes peered up and through us as if we were spawn of the devil. For all the other passengers knew, we were some horrible security risk walking among them and down the aisle. You want to embarrass a tween? Make him walk a gauntlet of shame all the way to the very back of a plane. I think Jimmy wanted to take that jacket and use it to completely cover his head—and probably would have if he could've done so and still seen where he was walking.

As we finally reached row thirty-four, Greg stood up to greet us, starting with the words,

"What the..."

"Don't. Say. A. Word. Not a word. I'll explain it all later." The Hubs is usually smart enough to know when it's not the right time to make a joke. This was one of those times.

"Well, folks, it looks like we're finally cleared for travel," noted the pilot over the loud speaker as Jimmy and I hastily took our seats, stuffed our bags under the seats on front of us, and fastened our seatbelts as quickly as possible.

"I'd like to welcome ALL our passengers onboard. We'll be departing the gate immediately. Flight attendants prepare for departure." To his credit he didn't call us out directly. I guess he could have added, "and the two high-level security risks sitting in row thirty-four will be available for your condemnation throughout the flight."

I learned a few life lessons from this experience:

– Sometimes it's better to keep your mouth shut and let others fight your fight.

– There is usually a douche nearby who wants to prove a point.

– Always move forward, never backward.

– When in doubt, be polite, smile, and say sir, ma'am, and thank you.

To this day I have no idea if the jetway onto airplanes is indeed a no man's land. If you risk it, and go backward, please let me know how it works out for you.

Bargain Master

I AM NOT FEARLESS. Nor am I a daredevil. I do not understand concepts such as jumping out of a perfectly good airplane, swimming with crocodiles or bungee jumping. I have a genuine fear of ending up as a winner of the Darwin award for attempting anything that would validate removing me from the gene pool. This doesn't mean I don't like to have fun. It just means I generally shy away from activities that require great heights, excessive speed, or hurling to my death in any way, shape or form. The twirling teacups ride at Disney World is about the limit for what my body, and psyche, will tolerate.

My dad is the same way. Both of us stand nearest to the door and face forward in those transparent glass-front elevators that sometimes operate in the middle of high-end hotels. That plexiglass platform at the Grand Canyon, the one everybody thinks is so cool because you can stand on it and see all the way through to the bottom of the canyon? Yeah, not going to happen for us. We don't do roller coasters. We don't do Ferris wheels. He has, to his credit, ventured up in a hot air balloon; well that makes one of us.

My dad seeks his adventures in different ways. He loves the thrill of the hunt—the bargain hunt. He's a champion estate sale junkie (has taught me all I know about the art of the ten-dollar haggle), a shopper extraordinaire. I've seen him make car salesmen weep, and he's never met a sales tag he can't negotiate down to a lower price. These are the skills that got us into an interesting predicament in, of all places, Roatan.

Roatan is part of the Honduras Bay islands. It's small, a mere forty-eight miles by five miles wide. It's become a popular stop for cruise ships on their western Caribbean treks and tourism has taken over as its number one industry, surpassing commercial fishing. It was by way of a family cruise that I and my tribe found ourselves on this beautiful little spit of geography.

Here's the thing about my dad: for him, part of the thrill of arriving in port is venturing out to find the one fantastic bargain that no one else has discovered. He's amassed a remarkable collection of gleaming wooden bowls and statues, sparkly jewelry for my stepmom, Mary, and numerous one-of-a-kind art pieces from their frequent travels abroad. Above all, he never books an onshore excursion through the cruise ship. Oh, no. He derives great pleasure in seeking out and negotiating a tour from one of the "locals." Thus would be our fate in Roatan.

As our eight family members walked down the ship's gangplank, Dad and his partner in crime, best pal Al, began to scan the dock and assess our options.

"Remember," noted Dad, "the guy I talked to (Dad always has a 'guy he talked to') said don't use the taxis or vans at the dock. Instead we gotta go to the left and out through the iron gate."

Sound sketchy yet?

As we ambled onto the cement pier, dozens of drivers spread out across the platform, holding up their *for hire* signs, calling out to the tourists who walked among them.

"Want to see the island? Come with me, just forty dollars for your group."

"Come with me, I know where Sylvester Stallone lives."

"Cool cab. I have bottled water, too. Will give you a good price."

Others from the ship moved on to the right toward a small town square where cruise line-sponsored, pre-arranged drivers were meeting their groups. I watched as Dad and Al turned in the opposite direction.

To the left, opposite the town square, was a dusty road, intersected by a black, wrought iron gate and fencing. The gate was open, and thirty feet or so further down the unpaved roadway was a lineup of battered and worn cars and vans, drivers leaning back against the rear bumpers, observing cautiously as the more adventurous tourists walked through the gates and down the path.

"Dad, are you sure..."

"Yep, this is what the guy told me; this is the place to find the best deal on an island tour."

"Okey dokey."

Dad and Al approached a tall, thin black man, dressed in a white button down short sleeved cotton shirt, the kind you leave untucked. His pants were black and simple, hanging loosely down to the tops of leather sandals. He had a broad smile and a friendly face, which showed promise. His vehicle was an old white VW bus, with tires that didn't look to be too worn, windows that were clean and open—an immediate indication there would be no air conditioning—and bench seats.

Soon, Dad and Al were waving us over to join them.

"Hello, everyone. I am Edward. Paul has asked me to take you on a tour of our fine island. It is going to be a good day."

In addition to my husband, Greg, with us that day was my dad, Mary, Al and his wife, Nancy, and, most importantly, my Uncle Gene and cousin Geno. Why most importantly you ask? Because I was about to discover the only thing in the world that could ever trump my dad's aversion to anything dare devilish, is his stubborn Irish resolve to never be one-upped by his big brother.

We piled into Edward's worn but clean van, settled onto the gray vinyl bench seats, and began our journey across Roatan. The island scenery was indeed beautiful. I was only occasionally distracted by the dice swinging from the rearview mirror, or the rumble of the van engine that sometimes seemed to struggle a bit to make it to the top of a sloping mountainside roadway. As we curved around and about the hills, you could look out across the lush foliage all the way back down to the port and the beautiful blue-green sea water. Sometimes we passed new construction of what looked to be fairly high-end villas. I got the impression Edward was showing us the nicer side of his neighborhood.

Edward, as it turned out, was a wonderful, friendly guide. He chatted with all of us and worked to learn each of our names. We stopped at a local store for waters and sodas and across the street, by coincidence I'm sure, was a small purveyor of local goods. Shockingly, Edward's sister and brother-in-law owned this shop. Simply shocking. I did purchase a beautiful wooden salad bowl that I still use to this day.

A little over an hour into our tour—which did, by the way, include the driving by of what was identified as Sylvester Stallone's house—Edward asked aloud if we would be interested in going to a local zip line operation. This was not included in the cost of the tour, but Edward knew a perfect group where he could get us a good price.

To my surprise, Dad replied, "Sure, we can take a look."

I made eye contact with Dad, and raised my eyebrows. Dad smiled slyly and shrugged his shoulders.

Edward's van turned down onto a rougher dirt path and pulled up to a thatch-roofed hut with a main counter in the middle, and benches surrounding the outer half-walls. Several men who looked to be mostly in their twenties were either sitting on the benches or leaning against the back wall of the hut.

Edward exited the van first and strolled over to where the others were gathered. As we approached, Edward was talking to what appeared to be the owner. I wondered if this was also a relative; a cousin perhaps?

"These folks are interested in your zip line," announced Edward. I was sure we were not the first group Edward had brought to this makeshift establishment.

The owner quickly produced laminated brochures which we passed around our group. Across the pages were photos from atop a high mountain illustrating a series of lines that hopscotched back and forth through the canopy. One photo depicted a smiling woman, trussed up in a harness and helmet, a cable reaching from her waist up to two cables above her head. She looked like she was about to step off the mountainside—and she was smiling!

As we intently reviewed the brochures, I discerned that the family members seemed to be waffling. Mary pronounced she would do whatever the group wanted to do. Edward's owner friend, sensing our hesitation, noted there was a long zip line course and a shorter one. Perhaps we would like to try the shorter which was a bit easier? We all still hesitated.

Abruptly, my Uncle Gene pulled up all of his eighty years, turned to the group, and pronounced,

"Come on, you bums. We're doing this."

He walked to the counter, said he wanted the long zip line ride, and noted we would all be doing the same.

And, that was that.

There was no way Dad was going to let his big brother show him up. Honestly, how would Dad have ever lived it down if he had stayed behind as Uncle Gene had gone careening down through the treetops without him? Dad leaned in, took my elbow and whispered, "Well, darling, after you."

After each of us relinquished our driver's license (I guessed to be used to identify the bodies) and forked over the seventy dollars, we were fitted for harnesses and helmets. Nothing, and I mean nothing in this world is less flattering to a middle-aged woman's ass than a harness that wraps around and through your legs and secures tightly around your waist. The bright yellow helmet and chin strap was a nice additional fashionista touch.

We next loaded into two separate Jeeps that would squire us up to the top of the highest hill, where the first zip line launch was waiting. The drive up to this location was not a good start to this adventure. Deep crevices and large potholes in the unpaved road made the trek extremely precarious. We were dramatically bounced and jostled about as we hung on for dear life, grabbing onto anything stable in the Jeep to keep from spilling out onto the rocky terrain. Sporting all that gear made the drive even more uncomfortable. The driver kept repeating, "It's just a little farther." That may have been the only English he knew.

Finally, we arrived at the top of the mountain. Three young men were waiting for us, each wearing his own zip line gear, and talking to the two others in Spanish. We cautiously got out of the Jeeps and walked gingerly over to where the mountainside seemed to taper off. Two long, thick cables swung overhead, attached to one of the large trees, angling back down and out over the tree tops, ending at a platform down below that looked to be as far away as the moon.

"OK, let's check all your gear."

Each one of us was inspected and re-fitted, adjusted and pulled tight, our helmets once again fastened snuggly beneath our chins.

For the first time, I checked in on the Hubs. Not surprisingly, he was standing at the back of the pack, taking pictures and video (there is good reason why a favorite family moniker for him is "photo boy").

"No way to chicken out?" I asked.

"None whatsoever," he replied. "A trek back down the hill in that Jeep would be way more dangerous than those cables."

He had a point.

One of the zip line fellas, the smallest of the three, lifted the harness strap dangling from his waist and connected it to a sturdy metal clip and mechanism that was connected to the overhead cable.

"My friend here is going to show you how easy this is," pronounced what I assumed to be the guide in charge. "All you have to do is take a few steps, lean out, and let the cable do the rest as you enjoy the ride," he cheerfully noted. "He will be on a single cable, but you will be connected to two cables."

The small guide took a few quick steps and then sailed out along the cable and down toward the next platform. He had made it look quite effortless, and a bit terrifying.

"OK, so, who's going to go first?"

Dead silence. All you could hear was the rustle of the foliage from the slight breeze way up high on the hilltop.

"Well, someone's gotta go first…"

"Alright, let's go," said Uncle Gene as he stepped to the front of the group.

"Great. Let's hook you up and send you down."

As we all watched silently, Uncle Gene—my gallant eighty-year-old uncle—took five brisk steps and launched himself out into the air, nothing underneath his feet but empty space and tree tops. I held my breath and listened to the whiz of the hooks moving across the metal cables as his harness carried him quickly down and out of immediate eyesight. Soon, a person on the next platform emerged and raised their hand to signal that Uncle Gene had safely reached the designated target.

My cousin Geno took the trip next, whooping and hollering the whole way down.

Each member of the group cued up and traveled down until the only ones left standing on the platform were Dad, me, and Greg, who had stood back and filmed it all for posterity.

"Well, Dad, who's it gonna be next, me or you?"

"Well, I can't very well let you go before me," noted Dad. With a wink he added, "I'll see you downstream."

Dad was hooked up to the cables, took several unsteady steps and then cautiously floated himself out along the lines. His hand held tightly to the harness cords as he rather awkwardly swayed out and down the course. I don't remember hearing any whoops or hollers, only the whizzing sounds of the zip line.

Turning to Greg, I questioned, "You aren't going to wimp out, are you?"

"In this family, are you kidding me?" he responded. "I'll be right behind you, right after I get your first zip line experience on film." He added with a bit of an evil grin, "Honey, your ass looks fantastic, by the way."

I was not particularly fond of him at that moment.

This was it, I was going to have to do this. The guide affixed my harness strap to the cables above and reminded me to try and relax and let the lines do the work. Taking a deep breath, I tested the line a bit by shifting my center of gravity back a bit and allowed the line to support more of my weight. This caused my feet to lift ever so slightly as my body began to move forward somewhat. I reacted immediately by drawing my weight back up and replanting my feet back down on the ground.

"Remember, try to sit back and relax," encouraged the guide.

I took three small steps and stopped again. Peering back at Greg, he smiled wryly, without looking up from the camera, and made a pushing signal with his free hand. I turned back around, gripped the straps tightly, and once again let my weight shift down into the harness. My feet dragged along the sand and gravel until I ran out of dirt and swung out and off the ledge, as awkward as a cow on roller skates.

The guttural yell that came forth from deep in my soul is the closest I've ever come to what I believe would be classified as a primal howl. But, I must admit, once I got past that first doozy of a step off into the unknown, and settled down into the ride, it was exhilarating! I ventured to take a look below and I could see all the beautiful Roatan foliage spread out in a flourishing multi-colored carpet. Gazing out to the horizon, beautiful blue sky served as back-drop to the lovely hillside slopes. I twisted somewhat as the wind caught my feet and turned me on a slight angle, changing my visual perspective somewhat. I could now see how the lines affixed from left to right across the mountainside, from platform to platform, all the way down to the bottom. Before I knew it, I glided onto the next platform and turned to see the guide signal that it was safe for Greg to take his first zip line trip.

The entire experience was invigorating in that you had to be willing to let go of control over your surroundings and your own personal well-being. As we each traveled from platform to platform, we became more confident with the procedure and our techniques improved. By the last line several of us were going down head first, or on a single cable. We laughed and joked about being such weenies in the beginning and reveled in the fact that we were now self-anointed zip line bad asses. What will always stay with me is that it was my dear uncle who goaded us young'uns into taking the risk. Thanks, Uncle Gene, we all owe you one.

At the bottom, we walked back toward the hut on a shaded path and as we approached I spotted Edward, sitting among the other men, laughing and drinking a soda. He stood up as we neared and grinning broadly, said,

"I see your smiles, so it was good, yes? Edward knows how to take care of you."

Indeed he did.

Exploring Roatan by way of bargain basement tour guides and zip lines may not be everyone's cup of tea. I'm not sure I would recommend my dad's methods to the faint of heart. Nonetheless, there's no denying he has a gift. If you ever need any tips, give my dad a holler. I'm sure he would love to help you find the very best deal.

D Day

I'VE BEEN THINKING a lot lately about the passage of time. Why is it that as I get older, time seems to move by at an accelerating rate? I've been wondering: Is it just me, or do others sitting here in the middle-aged cheap seats feel the same way?

Most research seems to suggest that my perceptions of time have a lot to do with where I am in my life cycle *and* what increments of time I am measuring. In time perception studies, adults in mid-life — *moi!* — report that the hours and days pass at what seems to be a normal speed, it's the *years* that seem to streak past us. I can attest that these first 50+ years flew by much too quickly and time now seems to be catching up with me. What is it they say? "It's not the years, baby, it's the mileage." Lately, I've been feeling both the years *and* the mileage.

I used to think I could get away with shaving a few years off my age and it not being completely unbelievable. However, recent passing glimpses in the mirror have me pondering: *Wow, I can't even pass for even five years younger than I am*. Vanity aside, the years have brought some wisdom and a lot of laughs; I just wish things would slow down a bit. I do love this quote from the great Albert Einstein regarding the passage of time:

"Put your hand on a hot stove for a minute, and it seems like an hour. Sit with a pretty girl for an hour, and it seems like a minute. *That's* relativity.""

No aspect of my life has seemed to pass by more quickly than the uber fast-paced years I've spent with my son, Jimmy.

I honestly feel like it was only yesterday when my son joined me in this world; a beautiful young soul, he has shared with me far more than I will ever be able to teach him. I blinked, and here he is today charging his way through graduate school. How is this possible?

I'll admit here and now that the physical separation six years ago from my only child was one of the most difficult experiences of my life. Time had flown by much too quickly. The years from diapers to kindergarten to driver's license to dorm room hurried past like the steady rush of a river.

The last year of high school, before Jimmy flew out of the nest, was a wonderful yet challenging time. In the midst of handling all the college prep "stuff," I worked hard to not lose the focus that this last year of secondary school was a time when many lifelong memories were made. Homecoming, band competitions, senior pranks, prom, and graduation parties all happen along the trail our children hike toward becoming independent. Jimmy was evolving into his own person before our eyes. Yes, all the typical high school anxieties were there but he was also developing an engaging, outgoing and funny sense of self. This sometimes included the bumping of heads as he tested his boundaries and we pushed back as necessary. I'm forever grateful for the midnight curfew enforced by Fairfax County which helped alleviate almost all negotiations regarding expectations of being home by a certain time. Other issues were not resolved so effortlessly, but for the most part it was easy to stay positive and enjoy the ride.

To be honest, as Jimmy sailed through his senior year, ever present in the back of my mind was this unequivocal fact, scratching its way to the surface: *He's going to be leaving soon.*

Each seminal moment began to bring us closer to the inevitable. The college campus visits in the summer morphed into application submissions in the fall. The obsession with taking the SAT and ACT exams at the end of his junior year switched to preparing for the upcoming AP tests. I began to keep a running list of "lasts" in my head: last football game, last band trip and concert, last high school spring break. When the college acceptance notifications began to arrive I was both elated and scared silly by his options. It was not a matter of if he would be leaving for college, but a question of how far away he would be going. His decision: Penn State, a wonderful choice and a mere four hours away. However, the decision to attend Penn State was simply the jumping off point.

The summer after high school graduation was filled with hundreds of small decisions, all contributing to D Day: Dorm Day move-in. More campus visits, and class scheduling, and roommate choices, and placement tests, and all the while trying—helplessly trying—to not be a gigantic helicopter mom. It's a tightrope we parents must walk: You don't want your child to go careening over the cliff's edge, but you do want them to have the adventure of deciding how to climb down the cliff without killing themselves.

When the day arrived to move Jimmy into his dorm room, I thought I was completely prepared. I believed I could fill the day with so many busy tasks that I wouldn't have time to let the thought—*he's leaving you*—fully bubble up to the surface. It almost worked. Right up to the moment when we needed to let go. My chest still tightens as I recall that difficult send-off:

I cannot breathe. I stand awkwardly in the parking lot, unable to force air into and out of my lungs. One of the greatest loves of my life, a person I've held onto as tightly as possible for the past eighteen years, is leaving me. As much as I've tried to prepare for this day, a day I knew was coming, I'm now paralyzed, unable to speak or think or breathe.

He's scared, too. I can tell. He's also eager to get this over with and I'm not helping matters. One last hug and he turns away, walking quickly up the sidewalk, swiping his newly acquired security ID across the keypad. I stand there helplessly watching as he disappears behind the dorm's front door and out of my sight. I'm certain my heart is about to burst right out of my chest.

Somehow I hold it together for the long, four-hour return drive home. But, once back, I am greeted by a place that is now much too dark and quiet and still. I walk into the family room and finally let it all go, crying so hard I don't think I will ever be able to stop.

This, my friends, was my first day as empty nester.

It became easier, but I did not immediately adjust well. My self-inflicted "Oh, I'm fine" public facade was neither healthy nor helpful. I was steadfastly certain that if I had shared what I was going through, I would've been greeted with snide remarks about cutting apron strings and getting a life and how this was the best thing for my child. I should have had more faith in my gal pals. I know now they would have offered, as they always do, support and encouragement.

As I look over on my kitchen counter and see all the glossy advertisements for college dorm room essentials and bargains, it occurs to me that maybe a few of my lessons learned from the lead up to and throughout that first year of separation might help someone out there who is currently hiding her fears and anxieties.

I'm no expert and I in no way profess to be anything other than a parent who has lived through the transition. Parent to parent, I can tell you this: It's going to be OK. Here are a few thoughts I wish someone had shared with me:

* Practice this mantra: "They are *away*, they are not *gone*." They are away, the same way they were away at camp or visiting relatives last summer. You will soon see them at Thanksgiving or parents' weekend.

* Do stay in touch, but don't "hover." Texting is your best friend. A random daily text lets you know they are OK, they are alive and up and out of the dorm. We are indeed fortunate to be parents in the technology age.

* Everything, in all probability, is not going to be perfect. The roommate may not be the best fit. Your straight-A high school

student may struggle a bit academically. That tennis team they thought they were a shoe-in to be selected for might not happen. If you also went to college, try to think back to your first year. It's unpredictable and a little overwhelming. As much as you are going to hate it, you've got to let your kid figure it out. I'm not saying abandon them—just the opposite. When they need your help, be there for them one-hundred percent, but it's a fine line you are going to be walking the first year.

* Your child will probably get homesick. Getting homesick is *normal*. The key is to discern homesickness from depression. I acknowledge, it can be a difficult call.

* It's OK for you to be sad, it's normal for you to be sad, but please don't let your sadness spill over to the point that your child feels guilty or worries unnecessarily about you. I'm not sure I was always the best at this. My son told me recently there were times when he worried about how I was doing.

If all goes well, and it most likely will, your child is going to have a blast. My son, in my opinion, had a life-changing college experience and continues moving forward in graduate school. He found his way, made great friends, and evolved into the man I always dreamed he would become. I love and cherish the time I now get to spend with him, but he's begun to have his own life and priorities—and it's great! I don't even cry anymore when he leaves after a visit. This did not happen overnight, but you will get there, I promise. If I can survive D Day, you can, too.

Magic Fishing Panties

THE BOAT ROCKS UP and down as the waves roll across the top of the ocean in an unrelenting waltz. It's a good day to be on the water; today Mother Nature is in a peaceful mood. I've been here more times than I would've ever expected. I'm no stranger to the ocean. When you grow up in Florida the beach and the sea are as second nature to you as breathing or laughing. However, this, *this* is different.

This is Alaska.

Back in 2005, I shocked the majority of my gal pals by announcing I would be heading to Alaska to go... wait for it... fishing. This crazy Southern Irish gal is a bit of a weird hybrid: loves pretty pedicures, but will also happily get downright muddy in the garden; will rabidly watch a football game, followed by her favorite DIY show on Home and Garden Television; is as comfortable wearing a frilly dress as she is relaxing in torn jeans and a sweatshirt. However, fishing?!

A little background: Nine years ago, the women in our family stomped our collective feet and demanded we be included in the annual Alaskan fishing trip. We had heard so many wonderful stories from the boys—husbands, fathers, brothers, and sons all blissfully sharing descriptions of beautiful Alaska. They told tall tales of monster halibuts and ferocious king salmon, of breaching whales, giant sea lions, and lush, rugged coastal terrain.

We gals wanted our fair shot at the glory. The pushback was in fun, but a little serious, too: There would be no girly girls allowed. You had to pull your own weight, be down on the dock at oh-dark-thirty—no time for hair or make-up—manage your own pole, and "woman up." Game on.

I'm happy to share that all these years later the gals are still going strong. Trust me, I'm the last person who thought I would come to appreciate and look forward to an annual fishing trip. Have I gotten sea sick? Yep, but only once, and I was a trooper and jumped right back to my pole after I cleaned myself off. Have I been miserable cold, hunched over in the icy rain and wondering how the hell I got talked into doing this more than once? You bet. I've been so exhausted after a day's fishing I've sunk fully clothed onto the bed and fallen fast asleep, even with the eternal daylight of Alaskan summer beating through the window. And still, I keep going back.

Over the years I've come to master the Alaskan fishing lingo. This is a must in order to handle yourself on the boat and pull your own weight. Here's a brief tutorial, a cheat sheet if you will, highlighting commonly heard expressions on an Alaskan fishing boat:

King. The biggest of the salmon. Puts up the best fight. Also known as a Chinook.

Trophy. A big king.

King Slayer. Common nickname of Kim Dalferes.

Silver. Another species of salmon. Also known as Coho. Superb eating; most often used to fill the fish boxes.

Pink or Pinky. These little suckers can put up a fight! But they're throwbacks. Hang out near the surface of the water. What's used for the canned salmon you purchase at the grocery store. You don't want to travel all the way to Alaska to bring these back home.

It's a Dog. When you land a chum or dog salmon. Toss 'em back.

Brown or Black Bombers. Rockfish, so named because they hang out near the bottom of the ocean. Can be a bugger to reel all the way to the top. Make great fish tacos.

Flatty, Chicken, or Butts. Slang terms for halibuts.

Parking Lot. A common fishing hole where fishing boats hang out together.

Fish On. Shouted when you have a fish on your line. Also known as a "hook-up."

A Double. Two fishermen with fish on their lines at the same time.

A Triple. A rare event. Three fishermen with fish on their lines at the same time. Often followed by…

An "Oh S***" Moment. Lines crossing, going over and under each other; fish making runs all around the boat; a general sense of chaos. Usually wicked fun.

In the Boat. When your fish is netted and brought into the boat. If it doesn't make it into the boat, it doesn't count.

Comin' in Hot. No net, no gaffe (which are used for halibuts), just horsing the fish into the boat. Not recommended, but sometimes necessary if you are having an "Oh S***" moment.

Bird's Nest. There is an art to casting and reeling. Fail to master your technique, and you could end up with a bird's nest—when the fishing line spools out of control up and around the reel, coming to resemble a bird's nest. Happens to everyone; embarrassing to admit.

Thumb It. To guide the line as you're casting and releasing your line, you gently glide your thumb back and forth across the reel. Do this incorrectly, and you end up with a bird's nest.

Derby. Fishing competition, mostly friendly. Winning the annual family derby bestows upon you the right to brag incessantly for a year. Except if you are my husband; then you need to drop it. Right, honey?

Mooching and Jigging. Fishing techniques. Too complicated to explain the difference; you'll just have to take my word.

Keep Your Tip Up. Often yelled at fishermen when the mates are trying to net your fish and get it into the boat.

Gettin' the Stink Off the Boat. Describes some mornings when it takes a long time to get the first fish into the boat.

Man-gina. A device which is strapped around your waist to provide support for your rod if you are having a tough time bringing in a large halibut. Warning: Don't ever ask for the man-gina. Right, honey?

This Ain't My First Rodeo. Term often used by kid brother Scotty when the women on the boat are getting too bossy.

There is a magical feeling when you land a king. The pull on the line is heavy and immediate. The line makes a unique zinging sound when a king grabs your bait and works to plunge down into deeper waters. As your pole bends under the weight, even the way the fish shake their heads is a distinctive alert to the captain and first mate you've got a king on the line.

I've learned to let the fish play out. Your instinct might be to reel down hard and horse or drag the king to the boat. This rarely works and does nothing more than wear you out. The real trick is to keep the line taunt and let the fish go up and down as often as it needs to. When it's time to reel him up to the boat, you'll know it. Even I, often the girliest of girls, have come to love the distinctive tug of a king.

Here's a little secret that might explain my affection for the annual trek.

Each year, on our last day out, the fishing lodge hosts a girls-only boat. This has become the favorite day of the year for us. The captain and first mate have their hands full working to manage a boat full of gals, but we sure do keep them smiling. It should be noted that not all the boat captains over the years have fully embraced our gaggle of gal pal fisherwomen. Most—such as Captains Kevin, Guch, and Bones—have tolerated and even enjoyed our propensity for fun and some silliness. I can clearly recall one ol' salty dog who made no attempt to hide his displeasure about being saddled with, of all things, women who fish. Little Bro Scotty immediately christened this brusque naysayer *Pecker Ted*. To this day, if you are behaving surly in my family you are often greeted with "don't go acting like a Pecker Ted."

What I've come to appreciate about girls-only day is that we sincerely don't care how many fish we catch, which probably contributes to our frequent landing of the biggest catch of the day among the boats. Maybe laughter is not only the best medicine, it's also the best fish bait. We women also have a secret weapon discovered during, of all things, a bathroom break.

We gals possess one distinctive disadvantage out on the fishing boats. It's the head. For the guys, their need to relieve themselves is accomplished by a quick pit stop over the bow of the boat. For the gals, well, our equipment doesn't work that way. A woman's use of the bathroom on a fishing boat is a time-consuming process.

I use the term "bathroom" here with a bit of poetic license. Often, the facilities are nothing more than a bucket. You can take as many countermeasures as possible: limit the coffee consumption and definitely go at the lodge before you get on the boat. But, eventually, you gotta go.

How to Pee on the Sea

Step 1: The captain clears out the cabin for a little semblance of privacy.

Step 2: Layers of clothing (gloves, hat, scarf, rain slicker) are removed.

Step 3: The bibs must be unhooked, but—and this is important—you mustn't remove them fully because this would entail also removing your boots.

Step 4: Shuffle over to the cubby area under the bow. You're lucky if there is a cubby area.

Step 5: Back in, derriere first, drop the bib tops you've been holding up, unzip and drop your pants, followed by your underwear, and attempt to squat/land upon the toilet/bucket.

Step 6: Pull across the battered blue plastic sheet that is supposed to provide some modicum of cover.

Step 7: Pray the toilet paper is somewhere within reach.

Step 8: Anchor your hands and feet against the sides of the cubby to steady yourself as the boat sways and rocks.

Step 9: Proceed with, well, you know.

Step 10: Attempt to rise, remaining in a somewhat stooped position in order to avoid bumping your head. (I did not forget about the use of the toilet paper; I'm trying to keep this classy.)

Step 11: While remaining hunched over, attempt to pull up your underwear and your pants in the cubby. Damn near impossible.

Step 12: Pull back the blue plastic sheet and while once again attempting to hold up your pants and bibs, turnaround, bend over, and pull the lever which evacuates the contents of bowl.

Step 13: Turn back around, continue to hold up your bibs, and shuffle back out into the main cabin.

Step 14: Refasten your pants and your bibs, put back on all your clothing—rain gear, hat, gloves, and scarf—and head back out to fishing.

What could possibly go wrong?

My stepmom, Mary, had held out as long as she could. However, eventually, nature called. She mastered steps one through twelve with aplomb, but upon reentering the cabin, her bibs caught on her boot, also tugging on her yet-to-be-fastened pants. As Mary stumbled and reached down to untangle the orange slicker fabric from the top of the brown rubber sole, she proceeded to bend over and show off her…panties.

As we heard her exclaim "Oh, shoot!" we all turned and were presented with her leopard print undies. Not exactly the granny panties you expect your mother to be wearing.

"Mom!" exclaimed sister Chris, "What are you wearing?!"

Mary abruptly stood up straight, hiked up her pants and her bibs, and with a wonderfully wide smile responded,

"Oh, these ol' things? They're my magical power fishing panties."

"Well there's something you don't hear on the boat every day," snorted Captain Kevin.

"Why do you think I'm so lucky each year?" replied a still grinning Mary. "Because I've got my power fishing panties on. Tell you what, I'll get all you gals a pair for next year."

True to her word, the next Christmas all the girls in our group received a pair of magic fishing panties in our stockings. Somehow, Mary had managed to not only find leopard print undies for all of us, but they also were purple! I ask you, how could they not be magical? Each year, without fail, we all wear our magic undies under all our gear as we head out on our girls-only day of fishing. These silly little slips of silk have become our girl-power symbol and have indeed brought us great luck and good fortune.

Sorry, boys, but I don't think you could ever handle the power of the purple leopard print. The gals respect the enchanted properties of our magic undies and have vowed to use their charms for good, not evil. Above all else, we sincerely enjoy winning the fishing derby; go find your own damn mojo.

Often, we women are told there are things we cannot do. We are too old, too weak, not pretty enough, not smart enough … all of it absolute horse hockey. My posse of fishing women issues this call to action to the sisterhood:

Hitch up your magic fishing panties and get on the boat.

My lucky fishin' hat and magical panties sit perched on a coveted shelf in the middle of my closet, patiently waiting to be packed and ready to leave the lower forty-eight for another Alaskan adventure. Who's with me?

Fish on!

A shout-out to the captains and crew of Islandview Resort & Charters in Sitka, Alaska. Thank you for taking care of—and putting up with—my family for more than a decade.

KIMBA REFLECTIONS

You know you are getting older when you go for a mammogram and you realize it is the only time someone will ask you to appear topless in a film.

—Lucy Blackman, *Have You Heard the One About... Aging*

I'VE ALWAYS TRIED TO LIVE by the mantra: *I am who I am.* This doesn't mean I haven't worked to improve myself, my life, and my surroundings. Even in my sixth decade, I have plenty of room left for improvement. As often as I've reinvented myself, this gal has always remained connected to her Southern roots and Irish disposition. I may have faked my way into a boardroom or a cocktail party, but once folks get to know me they usually realize I'm not that nuanced. I'm loud, I swear much too often, and I stubbornly work at something until I get it right. What has come as a bit of a surprise to me is that I didn't anticipate my frame of reference to abruptly change when I joined Club Fifty.

Middle-age brings with it a particular kind of perspective. I look back and realize I've gotten myself into loads of tight spots and ridiculous situations over my lifetime. I seem to now be entering a phase when age and wisdom are starting to win out over youth and exuberance. I find I don't have to win all the arguments. Sometimes I let the jerk-face driver who just cut me off go along his merry way without so much as a single honk of my horn. Every once in a while I don't share my opinion, I simply let a friend talk and I listen. This doesn't mean I'm now relegated to quietly rocking on the front porch; I still have a ridiculous knack for getting into trouble. Just recently I was back in Tallahassee for a FSU football game and found myself in the middle of a bar fight. Like my dad says, "Sweetheart, you do seem to always be in the thick of it."

I don't harken back to the good old days, but I do fondly remember the occasions, often with my gal pals, that have made me laugh, and cry, when I've behaved less than maturely, but almost always with great gusto and enthusiasm. What follows are a few of what I like to call my "porch stories," glimpses of me basically making it up as I go along and hoping I don't profoundly screw it all up. God only knows what the next fifty years will bring.

Playing the Girl Card

BACK IN 1984, when I was in my senior year at Florida State University, criminology was not as popular a major as it is today, especially for women. I'm not exactly sure why. I guess the study of crime wasn't that glamorous thirty years ago, before the advent of *NCIS* and *Law and Order SVU*. I would estimate that in most of my classes the split was about twenty-five percent women, seventy-five percent men. I ask you, as a co-ed, aren't those odds kind of attractive? For added appeal, many of the male athletes were criminology majors. One in particular, whose name I will refrain from using so as to not incur any sort of lawsuit but I will say went on to play in the NFL, was extremely distracting in his dolphin shorts—if you came of age in the eighties you know what dolphin shorts are all about. He may be the only reason why I never missed a 9 a.m. class my senior year.

For me, criminology has always been a fascinating subject. At the heart of this discipline is the question: what makes people behave the way they do and what makes some people break social norms and act in ways that are unacceptable to society at large? I think many of the guys in the program had dreams of joining the FBI or Secret Service. I was always much more interested in the prevention of crime. How do you, or can you, prevent someone from becoming a criminal? After thirty years in, I believe the answer to this question is that crime prevention is possible, but it certainly is complicated.

To graduate, all criminology majors were required to complete a one-semester, forty-hour-per-week internship. This became quite competitive for those of us who wanted to remain in Tallahassee. The city back in the day was all of 100,000 and although it was, and still is, the state capitol, agencies where you could intern in Tallahassee were not numerous. For reasons I can't readily recall, I was determined to intern within a law enforcement agency, but not necessarily at the local level. This led me to the Florida Department of Law Enforcement, also known as FDLE, Florida's statewide law enforcement agency with headquarters in Tallahassee.

The mission of FDLE is to promote public safety and strengthen domestic security by providing services in partnership with local, state, and federal criminal justice agencies to prevent, investigate, and solve crimes while protecting Florida's citizens and visitors. This must have struck a chord with me, the idea of not only investigating and solving crime, but also preventing crime, right there in their mission statement.

The big rumor about FDLE back in the early eighties was that female interns were assigned to either the crime lab or the training academy. The guys were given internships where they would be able to work out in the field. I have no idea if this was a valid rumor, probably not. However, when I was selected to intern at FDLE I was ready to shake things up, if necessary.

On the first day I reported with four male interns to a conference room where we would be subjected to a group interview in order to decide placement for the next fifteen weeks. We were lined up in our swivel chairs along one side of a large conference table and across from us sat several men from various agency offices. Bureaus or departments that were represented included the crime lab, the training academy, the director's office, and something called the "Domestic Marijuana Eradication Unit." Ding, ding, ding, this last one became my target. After brief introductions, we started down the line with the over-arching question "What are you looking to get out of this internship?"

When it was my turn to speak, I started with a question for the group.

"I'm a little surprised there are no other women in the room. Do you have women working here at FDLE?"

Gauntlet thrown.

"Oh, of course we do. It's just a coincidence our agency representatives today happen to be all men."

"I see. I'm curious, are there any women working in the Domestic Marijuana Eradication Unit?"

"Well, no, not at the moment."

"Have you ever placed a female intern in the unit?"

"I'm not sure, but, no, I don't think we've ever had a female intern express interest in that unit."

"Wow, that's surprising. It sounds like a great place to spend the next fifteen weeks, I'm sure I would learn a lot."

Girl. Card. Played.

I noticed the director nod and make a few notes. The perspective intern sitting to my right tried not to glare at me, but I bet he was thinking *damn that was brilliant... bitch.* We continued on down the line, and each intern pitched their rationale for wanting a challenging opportunity, perhaps working in the field. No offense to the crime lab or the training academy, but at the time those seemed like desk jobs. We were all seeking a bit of adventure.

We were finally dismissed for lunch, being told our assignments would be waiting for us when we returned. As the five of us walked outside one of the guys leaned in and noted,

"I can't believe you played the girl card."

"Well, tell me you wouldn't have done it if you could have?"

"Of course, but ... well, hell, good for you."

As promised, when we returned from lunch there on the conference room table was the list of our assignments. Second on the list: *Kimberly Joyce: Domestic Marijuana Eradication Unit.* The next day would be the beginning of this life realization for me: If you're going to play the girl card, you better be prepared to go all in.

The guys in the unit, five total, greeted me cautiously and eyed me from a wary distance. They were polite, respectful, but were certainly skeptical about a young co-ed with big boobs and long blonde hair invading their boys club. First assignment: a little research project. The guys had been working over the past year, assisting local law enforcement agencies with searches, seizures, and arrests all centered on domestic marijuana production. They had accumulated a large file of reports which documented when and where their work had been taking place, but no one had the time to pull all the information into a cohesive report with an effective way to track their work and easily discern where they had been most effective or where their resources had been best utilized. My job would be to cull through the information in the thick file and try to develop something useful for the unit.

Challenge accepted.

Remember, this was circa 1984, before the advent of laptops, crime mapping technology, and PowerPoint. This would be an old-school project. The guys would be in the field for the rest of the week leaving me to myself, the project at hand, and my first test.

The following Monday, when my co-workers returned to the office, they were greeted by my handiwork—a giant white board I had used to make a large grid of all sixty-seven Florida counties, cross referenced with each month of 1984. In each corresponding square were two figures: number of seizure events, and number of plants confiscated. The top ten spots had been designated with a bright yellow square as background. As I was reviewing the chart with the guys, I noted that if they needed to track the number of arrests for each seizure event, I could easily add that data.

"You did all this in two days?"

"Yep." I bet they thought I would be culling through that file for at least a week.

"I didn't even know this information was in that folder."

"Yep."

"Where'd you find the white board and the rest of the supplies?"

"Called over to one of the interns in the training academy. Turned out they were getting ready to throw this board out."

"Hmmm. Nice work."

"Thanks."

Test one complete. Little did I know the next test would present a much bigger challenge.

The next week the unit had scheduled a trip to a clandestine area of North Florida where it was suspected a makeshift marijuana production area had been constructed deep in the woods.

"Do you think you're up to coming along with us?" asked the unit supervisor.

"Of course," I replied. Being allowed to ride along in the field was one of the reasons I had wanted this internship in the first place.

"Well, come prepared to be out in the field all day, dress accordingly."

"Oh," he added, "you won't be allowed to carry a weapon. You're only there to observe, maybe help out a bit if necessary. Got it?"

"Got it."

The next day I made damn sure I arrived early—up-before-the-sun early—and ready to be taken seriously. No make-up, outfitted with a sports bra and hiking boots, and hair up in a simple ponytail. Also packed myself lunch and a water bottle.

After driving for about two hours we arrived at the destination—a field off a dirt road which backed up to a swampy area. Local law enforcement greeted us with:

"We're not sure how they've been getting equipment into the swamp. We suspect perhaps they've been airlifting equipment and dope into and out of the middle area."

Airlifting? We didn't have a helicopter. We did have a small twin engine airplane that was circling above, working to pinpoint the basecamp of the pot growers. But, what were we going to do? No way was I going to airdrop from an airplane!

After pondering the situation for a few minutes, the guys decided the best plan of action would be to hike in on foot, using compasses and some direction from the boys up in the plane.

"Kim, you up for this? No shame if you want to wait in the truck."

Oh right! Like I could turn this down. It was show time and I needed to woman up.

"I'm in. Here to help." In the back of my mind I was also thinking: I wonder if I've just been set up? My first day in the field and we will be traipsing into a swamp? Come on...

The locals eyed me a bit cautiously and a few seemed to be sporting wry grins. I was sure they were thinking: *Who does this uppity college girl think she is? This should be good.*

Our initial foray into the area wasn't too difficult. The ground was boggy and I was glad I had listened to the guys about putting on bug spray. However, the further we progressed into the woods, the worse the conditions became. The soggy ground morphed into thick mud which crept up and around my boots. Soon we were splashing through shin deep water and I noticed the light-hearted banter within our little caravan had dwindled.

I glanced to my right just in time to see a colossal black snake drop from one of the moss covered oaks and land in the water right next to one of the agents who—not to be disrespectful—screamed like a girl.

This broke the tension and made all of us stop and have a good laugh.

"What the hell, you guys?! That sucker was HUGE!"

"Geez, Gus," replied the unit supervisor, Tom, "I thought it was *college girl* letting out that scream."

"Yeah, yeah, real funny. Let me throw a big-ass snake at *your* head!"

Tom turned back to continue, but not before he threw a small wink my way.

A little bit further in, a radio crackled with news from Charlie up in the airplane.

"Hey guys, you're keeping sharp down there, right?"

"What's up, Charlie?"

"Don't want to alarm anyone, but I swear I just spotted a panther in the area."

"Great, that's all we need," replied Tom.

A panther?! If this was some sort of a test of my fortitude, it was the most elaborate rookie test ever. Tom turned to me, looking dreadfully serious.

"Kim, you're not carrying a gun, so stay close to one of the guys, in case they need to fire a warning shot to scare off that panther."

"Absolutely no problem."

By the way, and in case you were wondering, there is such a thing as a Florida panther. Not everyone knows this. They do exist and they can grow into exceptionally large kitties in the Florida swamps.

The situation devolved into the epitome of "all-in." There was no going back to the truck. I realized it had been foolish to think this was some sort of test. This was real. This was dangerous. This was nuts.

For what seemed like an eternity, we trudged on, following the compass and the directions from Charlie who, from up in the plane, had located the base camp. As the cleared area came into view I noticed the guys around me tense up, their eyes darting quickly around for any signs of the entrepreneurs who had set up this little illegal venture.

As I walked up, I first noticed the gear—what looked to be light farming equipment, fertilizer, and hoses. Then, up past the cleared area, I spotted the crop of five-foot-tall *cannabis* plants. Damn, that was some good-looking weed. This is when it first dawned on me: How the hell would we be getting any of this stuff out of the swamp?

One of the guys produced a camera and began taking pictures to document the crime scene area. Next, we dismantled as much of the equipment as possible, working to destroy anything that would be left behind, stifling the growers' ability to use the equipment in any future attempts at an illegal harvest. This left us with the dope.

"Only one thing left to do. We'll need to carry as much of this out as we can," noted Tom.

Great.

We fashioned some makeshift harnesses out of rope we had found at the camp and each of us, including me, hoisted the dope bundles onto our backs. I did notice the bale I was given was a bit smaller than the loads the guys were carrying, but this was not a time when I cared about preferential treatment one little bit.

An hour later, we emerged from the swamp and back into the open field where we had started. We were surprised to discover a local news crew waiting for us. Let's make sure the picture is fully drawn: I was walking out of the back woods with a large group of guys, covered in mud and dirt across every inch of my body, hauling a bunch of dope on my back. This was not how I envisioned showing Mom and Dad an example of how their daughter was spending her college days. Luckily, I don't think they ever saw me in the background of the story on the evening news. Oh, and for the record, we never did spot the panther.

The next week I was walking through an FDLE hallway and the agency director was coming toward me walking in the opposite direction.

"Hey, you're the intern in the Domestic Marijuana Unit, right?"

"Yes, sir."

"Heard about the bust in the swamp last week. Also heard you were a real trooper. Keep up the good work." Then and there I knew I had been accepted.

From the swamp day forward, the guys treated me as one of their own. There were many additional field assignments where we laughed and cussed and I told the guys my favorite dirty jokes.

In the end, the FDLE internship turned out to be one of my best college experiences. The guys I worked with truly helped ready me to transition into the working world. My biggest life lesson here: speak up, step out, take risks and fully use the cards that life deals you.

Fast forward thirty years and I'm facilitating a session for a non-profit organization that focuses on law enforcement leadership issues. As I looked out over the meeting participants I noticed someone sitting on the right side of the room who looked vaguely familiar. Glancing at his nameplate positioned on the conference table in front of him I realized he was one of the agents who had been part of the unit at FDLE so many years ago. He looked similar, but was now an agency director. During the break, I made my way over, never expecting him to recognize me.

"Hi, I'm not sure you will remember me..." I began as I stretched out my right hand.

"Kim! Of course I do! You were one of our best interns, so much fun. I remember you were one of the guys, never expected any special treatment. You never played the girl card."

Life sure is funny.

Once Again, Naked in Public

BEST GAL PAL DANI has a knack, a gift actually, for getting me into situations where, for various reasons—mostly on purpose—I find myself… naked. I'm not talking scantily clad or barely-there see-through T-shirts. There is no gray area here. I quite literally mean Bare. Assed. Naked. In public.

> **Plaintiff** (*moi*): "If it pleases the court, your Honor, I enter into evidence Exhibit A: the Korean Day Spa."

> **Defendant** (Dani): "Objection!"

> **Judge**: "On what grounds?"

> **Defendant**: "The plaintiff knew full well that upon entering said establishment, disrobing would be required."

> **Plaintiff**: "In my defense, your Honor, I did not fully understand, until it was much too late, that said establishment utilized towels the size of postage stamps."

> **Judge**: "Objection sustained."

Plaintiff: "I further enter into evidence Exhibit B: The Luxor Hotel, circa 2003, Las Vegas, Nevada."

Defendant: "Again, objection!"

Judge: "Grounds?"

Defendant: "The plaintiff cannot hold me accountable for her behavior in Vegas. May I remind the court that this comports with the '"What Happens in Vegas (including being naked in a hot tub), Stays in Vegas'" precedent?"

Judge: "Objection sustained."

Plaintiff: "Well then, your Honor, I offer my last and final Exhibit C: naked on a street corner in Washington, DC."

Defendant: "Objection!"

Judge: "Grounds?"

Defendant: "The incident in question did not entail full nakedness. We were, in fact, only partially naked… on a street corner… in Washington, DC."

Judge: "I believe I'll allow this final evidence. Objection over-ruled. Please proceed."

The Mandarin Oriental Hotel in Washington, DC, is by far one of the most elegant establishments in the area. Situated on prime real estate adjacent to the Potomac, it offers stunning views of the city. The grand marble entrance provides a spectacular welcome to all who enter. You actually *feel* different the minute you walk through the large lobby doors and over the threshold. This hotel is but one of a handful of five-star hotels in DC. After all, our city caters to government, business, and tourist-type travelers. We're not exactly known for our luxury digs.

I had the good fortune to be asked to meet a friend for a drink at the lobby bar when the hotel first opened back in 2004. Trust me, she was buying. The majestic architecture blew my mind. I knew I wouldn't often frequent this grand structure; not on my working-girl budget.

Turned out, a full seven years would pass before I would return to this oasis by the river. While perusing a high-end glossy shelter magazine during a 2011 dentist visit, my eyes were drawn to an advertisement for a budget massage at the Mandarin Oriental Spa. OK, it wasn't described as a *budget* massage, but something akin to "the midday sneak-away sample-how-the-beautiful-people-live experience." Presented before me on the magazine page was something even a budget-conscious girl such as myself could try at least once. I eagerly purchased a spa gift certificate for Dani for her birthday (yes, that's how I roll for my gal pals). I was elated when she suggested we go to the spa together as a joint birthday celebration.

Dani and I were able to find a work day during the August dog days of summer when we could meet at the spa for our pampering session—a day when I could travel into the District, and she could take an extended lunch break to steal away from her downtown office. This was not a common occurrence for us. We are not the ladies who lunch. We are the women who eat at their desks and multitask.

It's necessary to note, for reasons that will soon become clear, the spa at the Mandarin Oriental is located on the lower level of the hotel. As we exited the elevator, we entered a long hallway with shiny beige marble floors, dimmed lights, and soothing music playing in the background. In this netherworld, you immediately wanted to speak in hushed tones. A beautiful, dark-haired woman greeted us at the spa front desk. She took our shoes and washed our feet in warm, scented water enhanced with tiny delicate purple orchids. Right from the start we knew this would be a memorable experience.

Our lovely escort guided us to an elegant, wood-paneled locker area where we were asked to change out of our work clothes and into the softest, most lavish robe and slippers I've ever experienced. The slippers even fit—no small feat for a gal with size 11 feet. Dani and I placed our clothes and valuables in our lockers, secured our locker keys on the provided wristbands, and allowed ourselves to be guided back to each of our respective personal massage rooms.

My masseuse, a soft-spoken beauty with dark hair and eyes, waited patiently in the hallway as I hung my robe on the hook on the back of the door, kicked off my slippers, and eased my naked body onto the heated table and in between the ultra-soft sheets. I snuggled in, face down, and waited for her return.

The music lightly tinkled in the background as the masseuse, now back in the room, began to massage a lovely lavender scented oil into the tight muscles along my shoulders and down my back.

"Do you work at a computer?" she asked.

"Yes, how can you tell?"

"Oh, I can always tell by the tension in someone's neck and shoulders. I'll spend some time on this area for you."

Fine by me. Ahhh...

There are few things in life as blissful as being transformed from a bag of knots into a plate of applesauce by a skillful masseuse who has mastered the art of applying the precise amount of pressure exactly where it's needed. As I laid there, face down, close to drifting off to sleep—she was that good—the table quite unexpectedly began to forcefully shift back and forth.

Lifting her hands away from my back, my alarmed masseuse proclaimed,

"That's not me, I'm not doing that!"

Tucking the sheet up and under my armpit I rolled over and up onto one elbow. The table was still rocking, and all the beautiful little bottles of oils and lotions on the shelves were tipping against each other and falling over onto the counter. Strangely, I knew immediately what was happening.

"It's an earthquake," I stated calmly. Where this epiphany came from I have no idea. I'm originally from Florida; I do hurricanes, not earthquakes. Nevertheless, somehow I knew with great certainty and clarity that we were in the middle of a genuine shaker.

"It's a WHAT?! This is DC, we don't have earthquakes here!"

My calm, sweet masseuse was suddenly sporting a bit of a Jersey accent.

The shaking came to an abrupt halt. Almost immediately there was a knock and before either of us could say 'come in' the door swung open. Standing in the darkened doorway, with the emergency lights glowing behind her, was an older woman whom I assumed was the spa manager. She stated most matter-of-factly,

"We have to exit the building immediately. We believe that was an earthquake, and we are concerned the building is possibly compromised."

"Um, don't mean to state the obvious, but, I'm naked here."

"Sorry, we have to get out NOW. Grab your robe and slippers and please exit right away." Without closing the door behind her, the manager moved on to the next room.

My masseuse bolted through the doorway and out into the hall. In the dim light I grabbed the robe, slippers, and key with the hopes of being able to retrieve my possessions from my locker. I hastily slipped on the robe, shoved a slipper on each foot and attempted to head left toward the locker room. No such luck. The manager was standing in the hallway, directing all of us to turn right to take the stairs up and out of the building.

To my left, Dani's voice echoed out, "Kimmee? You OK?" I turned to watch Dani ignore Madam Manager, dash down the hall to her locker, and grab her cell phone. Why she didn't grab all her belongings was beyond me, but I was grateful she had been able to at least retrieve her phone before the staff whisked us outside.

The bright August sun greeted us as we shuffled in our robe and slippers out onto the city sidewalk. Up and down the street government employees, lobbyist types, businessmen, and other various well-heeled and suited professionals streamed out onto the pavement. A communal conversation began to arise and move through the stunned emerging crowd:

"What *was* that?"

"Was it an earthquake?"

"In DC—no way..."

"Another attack, a bomb?"

"Did you feel the building move?"

"Cell phones are down."

Dani and I stood there a bit shocked, not knowing quite what to say. I finally grinned and proclaimed,

"Well darlin', you've managed to do it to me again. Naked. In public."

Dani and I began to giggle like two small children getting into trouble during church services. The absurdity of our situation was becoming quite obvious. We were almost completely naked, no money, no identification, and in possession of a cell phone which wasn't working. If things went further south, what the hell were we going to do? Looking around, it began to occur to me that everyone else also knew we were nearly naked.

"Dani, is it just me, or are those guys in the suits with the briefcases across the street staring us down?"

Dani circled around and then playfully replied, "Should we give them a show?"

I grinned and said, "Honey, we're already giving them a show."

I continued, "You do realize we're in a bit of a pickle here, right? Let's say the worst happens, these buildings come down and we're buried in the rubble. No identification. Naked. In the middle of the day. We'll be presented in the history books as the 'Earthquake Hookers.'"

After many tries, Dani was eventually able to get a few text messages through to—of all people—my husband. He confirmed that, in fact, it looked to have been an earthquake, and a pretty strong one, too. Upon hearing of our predicament, he responded: "You're naked? On a street corner? Surely a pillow fight is about to break out. Pictures, please."

Men.

We found ourselves completely at the mercy of the hotel staff who were doing their best to keep us informed, but truly knew as little as we did. We finally found a bench under a tree where we could perch and perhaps not appear so conspicuously out of place. Sitting there, we had to be careful the robes didn't fall open as more people starting exiting the buildings, marching down the sidewalk in front of us with the occasional sideways glance our way.

I attempted to summon my best *What are youz looking at?* stare. It wasn't compelling; a lot of the fellas smiled widely and leered back.

After what seemed to be an eternity but was most likely only a matter of minutes, hotel management came to our bench to inform us there was concern about the spa's location in a sub-floor level of the hotel. It might not be possible for us to return for fear that foundation damage might have taken place. I stared back at the manager with a bit of disbelief flashing across my face.

"You do realize, and if you don't you're the only person in a three block radius who hasn't picked up on this, all we've got with us are the robes and slippers the spa provided. You see our predicament here, right? All of our belongings are in the spa lockers... our money, our credit cards and keys.... our CLOTHES."

"Yes, ma'am, I'm aware of our situation."

Our situation, now that was funny. I damn near asked him to switch places with me. I pictured him quite fetching in the robe and slippers. I could carry the menswear look—I had for most of the early eighties.

After almost an hour of being on display for the public's viewing pleasure, we were allowed back into the spa to quickly gather our belongings, get dressed, and beat a hasty retreat. I have no idea how they decided it was safe to return, but we weren't interested in questioning their judgment. The spa staff members were incredibly apologetic—as if it was their fault! They presented us with gift certificates to use for a future visit, as well as a set of lovely oils, as a parting gifts. I would've much preferred the robe, but thought it would have been quite white-trashesque to ask.

As we once again exited the hotel, this time fully clothed, we could see the DC streets were visibly swelling with commuter cars, all attempting to exit the city simultaneously and get back to the suburbs. The metro was beginning to overflow as well. Had we learned nothing from 9/11? This time around it was, of course, not even close to being as urgent. Most folks, I suspected, were simply eager to get home and assess any household damage. Yet, just like 9/11, the streets of DC became one giant, interlocking traffic grid-lock mess.

Dani and I headed back to our cars—she having given up on any notion of being able to return to her office—and joined the long, slow trek out of the city. It took me over two hours but, to be honest, the trip wasn't as bad as I had expected. I was buoyed by the knowledge that I had weathered standing nearly naked on a big city street corner… in daylight…with nothing separating me from the working masses except a spa robe and slippers. The thought still makes me smile.

Plaintiff: "And so, your Honor, what say you?"

Judge: "Based upon the evidence presented, the defendant, Danielle, is indeed guilty of getting the plaintiff into some wickedly fun trouble. You have a true and trusted friend in Danielle. Consider yourself lucky."

I do, your Honor, every day. There's no one else I would rather be stuck with naked in public. Well, except George Clooney, and Ryan Reynolds, and Hugh Jackman. Ya know, I might need to make a list …

* * *

This essay was the winner of the 2014 Golden Nib Award for Nonfiction and was included in the 2014 Virginia Writers Club Anthology (published 2015).

Exposed Temptations

WOULD YOU LIKE TO KNOW one indisputable universal truth about women?

Birthdays matter.

If a woman tells you her birthday is no big deal, she's probably lying. On other occasions a woman will happily endure and even appreciate a purchased-at-eleven-thirty-p.m.-on-December-twenty-fourth ugly Christmas sweater (don't even pretend you haven't done this), a last-minute cheap box of Valentine chocolates, or a hastily assembled Easter basket filled with stale Peeps. Birthdays are different. To be clear: I do not subscribe to the weeklong "my birthday makes me the center of the cosmos" silliness. However, it's certainly not too much to expect one day, one special and thoughtfully planned day out of three-hundred and sixty-five, be set aside for the woman in your life. A warning to all men: never miss a woman's birthday. Never.

My husband, Greg, had promised he would be home soon. Unfortunately, the Department of Defense had decided otherwise. War is funny that way: It doesn't often concern itself with our small, yet important, life celebrations. Full of self-pity and cheap sangria, I sullenly and quite selfishly complained to gal pal Nicole that this unexpected tour extension would disrupt my thirty-ninth birthday (thirty-nine being that last hoorah prior to forty, before we drift into dressing and acting "age appropriate" territory).

"Well," Nicole had replied, "what's needed here is a spectacularly immature act. Something even Greg wouldn't have considered. I'm thinking tattoo."

A tattoo! Truly juvenile, ridiculous, and inspired.

I had talked about getting a tattoo for years. It had always been just that—talk. The same way you talk about getting your boobs done or taking a poetry class or quitting your job to go backpacking through the south of France. Such musings always sound like fun and worthy adventures, but so does kissing George Clooney; doesn't mean it's going to happen.

Yet, there I was, a few days later, thanks to tremendous encouragement and hand-holding from Nicole, sitting perched on the tattoo parlor table. As we deliberated tattoo designs, "Tiny," the hefty tattoo artist, rolled his eyes as yet again another middle-aged rebel wannabe searched for the perfect symbol to represent her life's being. Nicole and I hastily flipped through the book of glossy colorful images of skulls, fairies, and roses. None of the images spoke to me. I had this one chance to get this last irresponsible gesture right. What was I going to do, pick a smiley face?

Somehow we eventually settled on the image to be inked on the top of my back left hip. Nervously I dropped the waistband of my jeans and panties to expose where the tattoo would be drawn. For the record, few things scream mid-life crisis more than exposing the top of your droopy derriere to a total stranger and asking him—no, PAYING him—to leave an everlasting mark permanently on your backside.

Tiny, sensing my hesitation, went to work immediately before I could chicken out. I was surprised to discover the procedure was not as painful as I had expected. It felt like a series of not-so-terrible bug bites. I had been warned I might faint. Puull*eeze*, the whole process was a mere blink compared to childbirth.

One fateful oversight was that I had forgotten to stop by the ATM before our little tattoo adventure. I was left with no option but to use my credit card to cover the costs. Thanks to modern technology, even though the military had stationed Greg halfway around the world, he would be able to review online the monthly credit card bill summary.

I was pleased to discover the August credit card bill simply noted: "$75—Exposed Temptations." Greg pondered this purchase for months. He never once asked me directly about the charge. Oh, but he noticed, and he wondered. I know this because he is smart, but he is not so smart. Casual questions were dropped such as:

"So, did ya do anything fun for your birthday?"

Or…

"Just curious. Purchase anything interesting lately?'

My answers were intentionally vague, little more than, "Not really."

I can play dumb, but I am not so dumb.

Months passed. Eventually Uncle Sam brought Greg back stateside and our first November night together in almost a year, reunited as a couple, finally arrived. By then I had pretty much forgotten all about my August birthday stunt. I even felt a bit sheepish about being so "all about me." That's why I was a bit surprised when Greg whispered, on this first night reunion:

"Honey, you gonna show it to me?"

"Show you what?" I asked back demurely.

"Come on, let me see the little thirty-ninth birthday surprise of yours."

At first, I honestly wasn't sure what he meant. Then, as I realized what he was referring to, a great big ol' smile spread across my face, and I answered,

"Oh, you want to see *that*, do you? OK, close your eyes."

I hastily stripped off my clothes and stood there before him in nothing but my birthday suit.

"Open your eyes."

"Where is it?"

"It's right here, baby."

Eyes wide, Greg replied, "Right here… where?"

"Here." I cocked my naked thirty-nine-year-old left hip toward him in what I thought to be a most sexy gesture.

"It's my bad-girl tattoo. Do you like it?"

"A tattoo?! That's my exposed temptations surprise?!"

Smiling, he leaned over and peered closer. "It's so tiny…. You got a weed put on your hip? You can cover it with a dime!"

"It's a shamrock!" I cried.

"Why, so it is. Didn't know I was married to such a badass."

More than a decade later, my tiny shamrock still sits there on the top of my hip, our little green reminder each year to be grateful for another birthday together. It may not have been the "exposed temptation" Greg had been envisioning, but my tattoo sure has lasted longer than any slinky black lacy thingy. Best seventy-five bucks I ever spent. Wanna see it?

*   *   *

This essay was selected as one of the winners of the 2013 VWC Summer Shorts Competition and is included in the 2013 Virginia Writers Club 2013 Anthology (published 2014).

Buscapades

I HAVE BEEN KNOWN TO BE, on occasion, quite stubborn. For the most part, my tenacity has served me well. Once I'm in, I'm all in; loyal and committed to the end. Go big or go home, right? I often blame my Irish ancestry for my inability to back down from a fight or give up on an argument. There are times when I get myself into predicaments due to the fact that I am flat out hard-headed.

January in Northern Virginia is wholly unpredictable. Dreary, overcast skies and damp, chilly mornings can be mixed in with lovely sunny days perfect for donning your favorite boots and a fun red coat. The problem is that the weather can turn quickly. What often starts out as a nice day can end up as a miserable, slushy slog-fest.

As a Florida girl by birth, these winters in the upper southeast are particularly difficult for me to maneuver. I never seem to choose the right clothes. I'm almost always wearing too much or too little and I never choose the appropriate shoes. Many a pair of heels has been ruined by a rain/sleet mix that crept up on me. There was one time in particular when not only did I ruin my shoes, but my stubbornness and unwillingness to take my husband's advice damn near got me killed.

My work often requires me to commute into DC for meetings with clients and government agencies. On these occasions I usually take public transportation. The greater DC area has been ranked in the top ten for the worst traffic in the US. Our traffic is, in one word: miserable. Drivers freak out at the very mention of the dreaded word *snow*. We've been known to shut down EVERYTHING before we get an inch of snow.

The morning I needed to head into the city husband Greg was showing some concern about the weather predictions.

"Honey, they're calling for some nasty weather to hit this afternoon."

"Oh, please," I responded, "Look outside. It's sunny!"

"I'm telling you, this doesn't look good. How 'bout I drop you off at the metro so I'll have the Subaru and I'll pick you up this afternoon?"

Note to reader: My husband's fancy-dancy sports car does not do well in any type of precipitation. I get made fun of for driving my little dependable Subaru until the all-wheel drive looks to be necessary. Then, who's the queen of the road?!

"Fine, whatever. I'm telling you, it's going to be nothing. What time can you pick me up tonight at the metro?"

"Just give me a call when you're twenty minutes out, cool?"

"Fine."

Hubby dropped me off early that morning at the Vienna metro and it was a normal, uneventful commute. Upon arriving in DC, I came up and out of the metro to be greeted by cool, dry weather, perhaps a bit overcast. Surely, The Weather Channel had gotten it wrong this time—no surprise there.

Our meeting was scheduled to start at 9 a.m. and go 'til 4 p.m. Several of the attendees had traveled in from other states and we needed to maximize this one full day together. As the facilitator, I was responsible for keeping us on task, reaching our meeting outcomes, and interacting in a fun and meaningful manner. It was troubling that before the meeting even began, attendees were grumbling a bit regarding the pending weather predictions. I assured all that we would end in plenty of time for everyone to travel safely back home. What a bunch of nervous Nellies.

During the meeting lunch break several attendees began to approach me with weather alerts. Because our meeting was in an interior conference room, we had not been able to look outside. A quick visit to an exterior office revealed that whereas the day had turned a bit gloomy, it in no way looked to be an approaching apocalypse. The Weather Channel was predicting otherwise: snow and sleet heading our way starting early evening. A text from hubby Greg confirmed that he, too, thought the weather was turning. What a worrywart.

A quick huddle with the meeting attendees revealed a universal concern about the weather playing havoc on travel plans. Sigh. I had to give in. We agreed to end the meeting by 2:30 p.m. The taskmaster in me wanted to finish our meeting agenda, but I had to acquiesce to the fact that the preoccupation with the weather was beginning to distract all the participants. A facilitator has to be flexible, even if she is a Virgo.

True to my word, I ended our meeting at 2:30 p.m. and encouraged everyone to leave as soon as they could with safe travels to all. I remained behind to clean up the meeting space because I surely had plenty of time to get home.

An hour later, when I walked outside, I was greeted with the beginnings of the snowfall. The sky had turned the smoky gray color when it's heavy with snow and sleet. Slush was already accumulating on the sidewalks. Most certainly the wrong day to have chosen stylish suede boots. I would be regretting my shoe selection many more times over the ensuing hours.

When I entered the Metro Center station I immediately noticed the underground platform was quite crowded—silly people! I was sure they were all hurrying out to buy mega rolls of toilet paper and gallons of milk in preparation for a mere dusting. I could not have possibly imagined what would be in store for me at the other end of the Orange line.

I quickly saddled myself into a window seat on one of the vinyl red benches. As the doors of the metro door closed and we pulled out of the station I thought to myself: *All is not lost. The client will be happy with our progress today and I might even be back home in time to go to the gym before dinner.* Silly me.

The orange line of the DC metro system, when heading west out of DC, does not reach above ground until it snakes upward right outside of the East Falls Church metro station. Why is this important? Because for several underground stops and almost half an hour I was out of touch with the outside world. As we moved forward, a bit slower than normal, the announcements from the train operator began to sound a little ominous:

"Sorry for the brief delays we are having folks. The above-ground tracks have become a bit slick so we're slowing down the trains as an added precaution."

Uh-oh.

When we surfaced outside of East Falls Church it was if we were exiting out the other side of a black hole. The snow was blowing so hard it hit the train sideways with a gusto significant enough to create a resounding thud against the metro car window. I couldn't believe my eyes—we had left the city less than thirty minutes ago! Visibility was less than a few feet. The universal reaction in the car: holy sh**!

I took out my phone to find I had four unanswered messages from Greg. Poor guy, he was probably sitting at the Vienna metro parking lot, wondering where the hell I was. Without listening to any of his messages I quickly dialed his number.

"Hello?"

"Hi, honey. So sorry I didn't pick up when you called, I've been on the metro and we just got above ground. Very sorry you're waiting for me at the Vienna metro in this weather. Are you at least in the parking garage?"

"Oh, I'm in the parking garage… at my office."

"What?!"

"I guess you didn't hear any of my messages. I'm stuck. We can't get out of the garage."

"Are you kidding me? Come on, it can't be that bad…"

"Why would I make this up? We're snowed in. I suggest you turn around and head back into the city."

"What?! No way, we just left East Falls Church. Are you sure you can't get out?"

"Yep."

"Well, I'll take a taxi home."

"Honey, listen to me, no one is getting anywhere. There will be no taxis! Your only option is to turn around and find a hotel room in the city for tonight."

"That's crazy! I'll get home."

"Not going to happen, I promise you."

"Well, I'm going to make it home. I'll check back in with you when I'm in the cab."

"You need to listen to me…"

"Will call you later." Click.

Yep. Stubborn to a fault.

Unfortunately, I quickly ascertained that a cab was not going to be an option. Upon arriving in Vienna, I walked out of the metro station and was greeted with a blast of frigid air as the snow continued to blow sideways into the departing crowd. The ice and slush was piling up quickly and ad hoc lines were forming everywhere as commuters desperately tried to figure out an exit strategy. I was about to admit defeat and return into the station to take a train back into the city when I spied it. Off to the side, with a line waiting to board, was a bus with its glowing sign beckoning: Fair Oaks Mall.

Salvation! The Fair Oaks Mall was at the most five miles away. I could hop on this bus and wait out the storm surrounded by the comforts of mass consumerism. I had visions of martinis and Chicken Caesar Salad mixed with leisurely boot shopping to replace my current pair, which were now becoming quite sodden and ragged.

Putting my head down to shield my eyes from the blowing sleet, I staggered over to the bus and was lucky to be one of the last people to board. Only three people behind me were allowed to step in and then the doors closed up. It was dry and warm here in our bus cocoon. I sat down next to a friendly looking woman who nodded her hello. We shared relieved looks conveying we had managed to find this refuge.

And then, we waited. And waited. And waited. The bus did not move.

Passengers began to gingerly ask the driver when we would be leaving. These early attempts to communicate with the driver, the woman who occupied the seat of power, were ignored. Though no one wanted to risk pissing her off, after an hour it began to look like our clan of commuters was quite close to executing a bus takeover plan. Finally, after many ignored inquiries, she said aloud to no one in particular:

"Can you see this parking lot? I got nowhere to go. Trust me I wanna get out of here too, but I can't get past all the cars piled up from here to the stop sign."

She had a point.

Fifteen minutes later, quite abruptly and without notice, the bus lurched forward—mere seconds away from a hostile coup I can assure you. Unfortunately, we only moved about ten feet from the curb and stopped again. This starting and stopping and inching across the parking lot would continue for the next two hours.

Sporadic communication with Greg continued. He had given up all hope of making it out of his parking garage and had retreated back to his office along with his colleagues. He wasn't too pleased to hear I was now stuck on a bus. The words *I told you so* were never uttered, but they were certainly implied.

It occurred to me that perhaps I should take inventory of pro-visions. Being that it was almost 7:30 p.m., I was beginning to get hungry. A perusing of my purse turned up a stray linty lifesaver; a year-old Twix bar; a half-roll of sugar-free mints; an energy bar— YEA!; airplane peanuts—damn they looked old; and what seemed to be a piece of butterscotch candy, but could have also once been a pretzel.

I became fascinated with the actions of my fellow passengers. Slowly, as individuals became discouraged by our progress, they began to ask the driver to let them off the bus. Where were they going? By now, hours into this adventure, the metro trains had shut down so the transportation options seemed quite limited. Cars were strewn in a haphazard manner all over the parking lot as drivers skidded into one another in futile attempts to reach the roads, which were equally as treacherous as the parking lot. A crazy rumor began to circulate that there was a McDonalds up around the corner which enticed several additional passengers to abandon our safe haven. I listened as another passenger negotiated a pickup at a 7-Eleven. A guy at the back of the bus was apparently married to someone named 'Lisa' who was not buying his story about being stuck on a bus. Had she heard this excuse before? Dude was in desperate need of some better alibis.

As full darkness descended, visibility from the seats in our chariot was reduced to zero. The windows fogged up and it became disorienting to not be able to see even a foot out into the blackness. The driver continued her futile starts and stops across the parking lot, but it was impossible to determine if she was making any real progress. As we approached our third hour on the bus, the driver announced we had finally made it onto the road that ran parallel to the metro station.

I peered out through the front of the bus just in time to see the car directly in front of us spin out. An audible *whoa...* passed through the bus. We were now facing the car head-on as if we were competing in a crazy game of chicken. Oh, and have I mentioned that as our third hour ticked by there was no bathroom on this bus? Yeah, thought I should throw that little detail out to you for good measure.

Several of the fellas on the bus got out and helped move the spun-out car over to the side of the road in the hopes that we could pass. The car's driver seemed to abandon all hope and left his car right where it had been moved, still facing the wrong direction. I watched as he thanked our small team of movers and walked up the road and out of sight.

As soon as we were all back on the bus the driver began to once again attempt to move forward. Our problem was this road was on a small incline and each time we seemed to gain some traction, we would inevitably slide backwards. She gunned the engine as best she could, which resulted in putting the bus into a fish-tailing side-to-side motion. Our collective "Whoa, whoa, WHOA!" put a stop to this maneuver fairly quickly. Unfortunately, the brakes did not hold and we slid backwards, coming to rest only after we sideswiped a BMW whose driver had made the not so smart decision to attempt to drive around us as we were sliding.

When we finally came to a complete stop our bus driver—who believe it or not we were all becoming quite attached to—pronounced to the group:

"They do not pay me enough for this s***!"

She then opened the bus door and disappeared into the darkness.

"Where the hell is she going?" someone asked.

"Um, I think she might be running away."

"She can't do that, didn't she take some kind of oath or somethin'?"

"She's not the captain of a ship, she's a bus driver. I guess she's had it."

One of the guys walked to the front of the bus and peered out the bus door which she had left open. Then with a snort he turned back to us and replied,

"She didn't abandon us, she's taking a leak in the woods."

"Well good for her... I gotta go too!"

"Well, if ya gotta go, you better go do it now."

I crossed my legs and held steady. Peeing in the woods, in the middle of a snow storm, with a bunch of strangers, was an experience I was willing to take a pass on.

After our little break, and when we were all back in our seats, one of the guys raised the idea that perhaps we could all get out of the bus and push. Our driver nixed this almost immediately.

"Ya'll ain't going to be able to push this bus. The last thing I need is ya'll back there slipping and sliding and risking me or someone else hitting you. You're not Keanu Reeves and this ain't the movie *Speed*, so don't even think about getting back out there."

She did care about us, or maybe she just didn't want to get sued. I seriously considered offering her my airline peanuts.

Around 10 p.m. our bus driver decided to give it one last try. We had learned she had kids waiting for her at home and she was as tired as the rest of us; maybe even more so in that she was dealing with the stress of trying to drive us out of this mess. We held our communal breath as she gunned the engine, removed her foot from the brake, and began to turn the steering wheel back and forth as we lurched up the small incline in front of us. At first it appeared we would make it to the top of the hill. Alas, the traction didn't hold and as we rolled backwards, the front of the bus glided around to the left and we slid sideways to land in the road easement, facing the wrong direction.

This last attempt was the deal breaker for everyone left on the bus, including our driver. Nerves were shot, stomachs growled, and many bladders still needed to be emptied.

As we exited the bus, being careful to step away as we maneuvered out of the embankment, we noticed the snow fall had subsided somewhat and we could make out some lights across the field. Someone noted they thought we were near a strip mall on Nutley Avenue. Sure enough, if you squinted you could see the sign for the *Glory Days* restaurant in the distance. The reality was that over the past five hours we had traveled less than a mile. I was never going to live this down with Greg.

We trudged down the road, the deep snow almost up to our knees, and arrived at the *Glory Days* front entrance in a matter of minutes. I'm happy to note we did not lose a single man during our treacherous crossing. Do you recall the moment in the movies when the front door of the bar swings open and all the locals turn around to size up the strangers who are entering *their* establishment? That was exactly what it was like when we walked through the restaurant front door. If someone had said "Ya'll aren't from around these parts, are ya?" it would have been perfect.

After my much-needed bathroom visit, and a well-deserved Jack and coke, I was able to connect with Greg to tell him where I had ended up. To his credit he didn't give me one bit of grief. He was still stuck at his office, but they had begun the process of digging out. He also noted that a good friend of his, Pete, lived around the corner from *Glory Days* and perhaps he could help us out and come get me. Greg seemed to remember that Pete drove a four-by-four and might be able to get around on the snow and ice.

True to his word, about an hour later Pete appeared to fetch me from my *Glory Days* oasis. I bid farewell to our bus caravan, including the driver who had joined us. She was a good woman. I regret I never learned her name.

It would take Pete and me another hour to navigate back to my house. Roads were littered with cars, many abandoned in the middle of the icy road. We also passed a fire truck in a ditch and five more metro buses, all of them still and abandoned. I noticed the weight of the ice and snow had also brought down many tree limbs across power lines, leaving some neighborhoods eerily dark. It was like something out of an apocalyptic movie.

As Pete dropped me off at the top of my pipe stem drive—no way was I going to ask him to attempt our steep driveway—up behind him drove Greg in my little dependable Subaru. It was a relief to see him. As we walked down the pipe stem together, slush now fully seeping through my ruined boots and brushing along my coat, he put his arm around me and asked,

"How was your day, dear?"

"Ah, it was alright. Nothing special. I might need to go shoe shopping tomorrow."

Apathy

Congress shall make no law respecting an establishment of religion, or prohibiting the free exercise thereof, or abridging the freedom of speech, or of the press, or the right of the people peaceably to assemble, and to petition the Government for a redress of grievances.

—*First Amendment, Bill of Rights, U.S. Constitution*

I'M A BIG FAN OF the First Amendment. Our forefathers showed excellent judgment in placing our right to free speech and assembly as *numero uno* in the Bill of Rights. Over the years I've certainly exercised my First Amendment rights and participated in my fair share of marches, protests, and rallies. A recent foray into peaceful assembly was participation in the Jon Stewart *Rally to Restore Sanity*. It was hot, crazy-crowded, and I could barely hear the speakers. I have to admit I would've been better off watching from home, or perhaps I'm getting a bit too old to be enamored by giant crowds and port-a-potty lines. It's the ideal I continue to embrace: In this country, everyone has a voice—even if some vehemently disagree with that voice. But, I ask you, does the right to free speech cross the line when it intentionally inflicts harm on others?

I was not fully prepared to be alone and once again a single mom a mere six months into my marriage. Of course, the events of 9/11 changed many lives, altered plans, and re-directed priorities. My impositions were minor compared to many.

Prior to meeting and falling in love with Greg I had no experience with living the life of a military family. Married in May of 2001, we had only four months of wedded bliss before 9/11 struck. When Greg, a reservist, was called up for active duty I was thrust into a strange world of military acronyms, powers of attorney, base access, and emergency contact protocols. By January of 2002 he was packed up and shipped off, and I was left behind to take care of and adjust to a new house, new school for our son, and a new job.

As a reservist family at the start of the mobilization, the built-in supports and camaraderie the military creates for its families were not readily available to us. It should be noted that, in the years since Greg's deployment, the military has vastly improved the support systems for their reservist families. In the first months of the massive reservist call-up post 9/11 all priorities rested on the immense mobilization — a *hurry-up-and-we'll-work-things-out-as-we-go-along* model seemed to be in place. It was not lost on me that the military powers that be had a few other priorities. A clueless military reservist wife was way down on their list of concerns.

I made a little deal with myself: I would make the best of things and I would work diligently not to complain. There were so many people who had lost loved ones and were sacrificing much more than my family. I needed to be grateful and to expend my energies supporting Greg and taking care of our son. I was not perfect. I did fall victim to feeling sorry for myself on occasion. Late at night, after Letterman, a king size bed can become a very lonely place.

By April it was becoming apparent this wouldn't be a short mobilization. My new normal was once again the life of a single mom, hustling to get myself and young son out the door each morning, coupled with dog walkings and lunch packings and rushing to make the train into DC. Most days I managed the usual array of commuting challenges — crowded and delayed trains, inclement weather, and often questionable substances found on metro car benches—with calm resignation. However, I was now also greeted each day by a new presence in DC that emerged over the months following 9/11: the war protesters.

As the throng of workers exited the metro station each morning and trooped toward their work places, we were greeted by earnest yet somewhat pushy protesters who eagerly waved their outstretched hands in the hopes we would take from them their mass-produced anti-war pamphlets. I was always a bit surprised by their age and appearance. Mixed in with the young, impressionable and somewhat righteous rebels were middle-aged, well-dressed men and women who were equally committed to the cause. My personal bias was that I expected the young to be passionate, opinionated, and headstrong. Older protesters, on the other hand, always got my attention. I wondered about their families and their jobs or the lack thereof. I don't begrudge anyone the right to express their outrage with clear conviction, I'm just always surprised when it's articulated by someone over the age of thirty. It was indeed one of these older protesters, a woman, who effectively turned my April morning upside down.

The art of maneuvering around any protest requires one to never make direct eye contact. When flyers are pushed your way a polite "no thank you" mumbled as you skirt around the demonstrator, is usually all it takes to appease the dissenter and allow you to move on. However, on this fateful day I was somehow singled out by the one woman who was itching for a fight.

I spotted her as I was coming up the station escalator. She looked to be in her mid-thirties, sporting shoulder-length frizzy hair and a large, worn canvas satchel of materials which hung cross-wise in front of her. Her non-descript raincoat fell to the tops of her sneakers, covering a long-sleeved T-shirt and jeans. In each hand she grasped papers which she diligently urged each commuter to take as they walked past. The few commuters who took her materials almost immediately dropped them to the ground as they skirted around her. I remember thinking she must have been getting frustrated.

As I walked past her, I heard her familiar spiel: "Stop the War, Stop Our Government, Stop the Slaying of Innocents…." I had indeed heard these rally cries many mornings since the U.S. had started sending troops overseas. As she pushed the contents of her hands my way, as always I muttered a faint "no thank you" and brushed past her to continue toward my office. It was what she said next that stopped me in my tracks.

"Must be nice to be so apathetic," she all but shouted at my back.

Stopping was a big mistake. She had baited me and I should have known better. I should have kept right on walking and ignored her. I should have done a lot of things instead of turning around.

"What did you say to me?"

"Apathetic. It means to not give a damn about your country," she shot back.

Admittedly, I have a bit of a temper facilitated by Irish DNA handed down through the generations. I've never hit another person, but I have had my fair share of verbal altercations and ugly interactions. I've often heard or read terms such as *my blood boiled* or *all I could see was red* or *I was so angry I could spit*. However, it was not until this interchange with this war protester that I gained a personal understanding of being furious enough to want to actually do bodily harm to another human being.

I wheeled on her as if she were Satan himself.

"You don't know me. You don't know anything about me! Who the hell do you think you are, calling me apathetic?!" I damn near spat at her.

She didn't miss a beat. She knew she had landed exactly what she had been fishing for: I would be her trophy catch of the day.

"So, tell me then, do you support this war?" she calmly asked.

"I don't have to tell you s***! My personal situation is personal. I don't owe you any explanation of what I do or don't believe in!"

"Why are you yelling at me?" she replied with a sly smile on her face. "I just want to talk to you."

"No you don't, you want to tell me how you're right and I'm wrong. Could you be more smug?! Apathetic? You have no idea how much this war is affecting me."

"Enlighten me."

"Go screw yourself."

What happened next was the worst, truly the worst possible thing she could have ever done: She laughed at me.

"OK, hothead, you go have a nice day working for the man."

At that moment I could have committed murder. I have never been so completely out of control with my reactions and emotions in all of my days. I could have easily pulled back and punched her in the face. What stopped me? To this day I'm not completely sure. She continued laughing as she walked away and back toward the top of the escalator, returning to her efforts to engage other commuters, leaving me standing there in front of the metro station with tears quickly springing to my eyes.

I had been oblivious to the small crowd that had stopped to watch our brief interchange. Feeling utterly humiliated, tears ran down my face as I watched people resume their daily routines and hurriedly move past me, as if to convey *we want no part of this, you're the idiot who got sucked in, you're as crazy as she is...* And they were right, I had been duped.

It was a short walk from the metro to my office, and yet it seemed to take me forever to reach the refuge of my building. I had begun crying in earnest by the time I reached the marbled lobby. When I exited the elevator and entered our office suite I walked past my own office and instead went straight in to see my Vice-President. I don't think I even knocked. Without removing my coat or putting down my bag I immediately launched into a description of what had happened. As my rant continued, my voice became louder and louder, intermixed with indignant sobs. Darryl, one of the best bosses I've ever had, didn't interrupt me, not even once. He calmly got up and closed the door. Even when the Director of Personnel called to ask if everything was OK—yes, I was making that big of a fuss—he quietly reassured her all was fine and to please ask the receptionist to hold his calls.

Slowly, I reemerged into the land of the sane people. After I had vented for at least a full ten minutes, Darryl managed to get me to take off my coat, sit down, and have a cup of coffee. With a calm voice and gentle disposition, he eventually helped me to realize that my completely out of proportion flash of anger was not only in response to the protester, but was also a response to five months of holding it all together.

"Kim, it's OK for you to not be happy with your current situation. It would be weird if you *were* happy with your life right now," Darryl noted. "I think you may need to admit that doing it all by yourself, well, it sucks. However, it might not be healthy for you to be expressing your frustrations by allowing yourself to be baited by random people on the streets of DC. I'm sure you could have taken her, but, I'd rather not get the call to post bail for you."

Have I mentioned Darryl was a great, exceptionally great, boss?

Days later I did everyone a favor and had a little visit with an Employee Assistance Program counselor. In a simple, one-hour session she gave me some great advice I've used more than once since my altercation outside of that metro station. In these types of situations, put down in writing what you would like to tell the person who has hurt you, dismissed you or insulted you. Write a letter as if it will be read by the one who has caused you pain.

I'll admit that at first this seemed to be a silly exercise, but as I wrote and refined my letter I found myself beginning to feel much more in control of my emotions and my situation. I've never shared this letter with anyone, until now.

Dear Anti-War Protester,

You don't know me, and you never will. I am one of the nameless, faceless people you address and confront each day. In your earnest attempt to have your views heard and understood, there a few things I wish you would keep in mind:

Your words, especially spoken in a taunting fashion, can be hurtful. I know you want to provoke a response. You want to be a vessel for change. But, that does not entitle you to be cruel. That person you just confronted, he or she may be having a difficult day, month, or year. In these trying times, please remember many are struggling. You shouldn't be adding to their struggle.

Most people respect what you are working to accomplish. We understand it's not easy to start up a conversation out of thin air with a complete stranger. Nonetheless, please respect the fact that we may not want to talk to you. We shouldn't have to defend ourselves. We are Americans, too, and we have the right to move past you without reproach. I'm guessing it's difficult to not take it personally when we ignore you. That does not give you the right to make it personal.

You do your cause a great disservice when you unnecessarily provoke or attack others. Remember, you are not only representing yourself, you are representing a cause. If you truly believe in that cause then the fight should never be about you.

Sincerely,
Just Another Face in the Crowd

After I wrote this letter and read it several times, I realized what I most wanted was another meeting with my assailant and a chance to attempt to have a calm conversation with her. In criminal justice circles this is known as *restorative justice*. Perhaps she didn't know anyone who was directly affected by 9/11 or the military call-up. Maybe the universe was looking to me to enlighten her a bit.

Alas, by the time I had mustered the courage to look for her, she was gone. For years now, whenever I'm in the city and I come across a demonstration or rally, I scour the faces of protesters, looking for her frizzy hair and worn canvas bag. I've never been able to locate her. I often wonder if she would remember me. Do you think she would be interested in how my life turned out over this past decade? Would she care that my husband returned home safely after his year-long deployment? I carry the hope that if I never see her again, perhaps she may somehow instead read this. So, dear protester, if you're still out there, leading the good fight and exercising your First Amendment rights, please believe I sincerely hope you have a good day and a good laugh, but not at someone else's expense.

Wax Job

A YOUNG SAILOR, after many months at sea, finally secures a weekend pass. He rushes off the ship and immediately heads to the nearest house of ill repute.

Knock, knock, knock.

The door swings open and a scantily clad woman appears in the doorway.

"How can I help you, son?"

"Hello, ma'am. I'm a sailor and I've been out to sea for many months. I've been told you are the woman to see for a little relaxation. Am I in the right place?"

The woman looks the sailor up and down and replies, "Why yes, dear, I believe I can be of some assistance. Please come inside."

The sailor enters and eagerly exclaims, "I want the very best you have to offer. Money is no object."

"Well then," the woman replies, "what you'll be wanting is a wax job."

"A wax job. I like the sound of that! How much does that cost?"

"It's $100, but I promise ya honey, it's worth every penny."

"That's a lot of money," notes the sailor, "but I did ask for the best." The sailor opens his wallet and hands over five twenty-dollar bills.

"Well done. Please follow me."

The sailor follows the woman into a dimly lit back room. Strange music is playing in the background, similar to the sound of wind chimes.

"It's very important you do exactly as I say. OK, sugar?"

"Yes, ma'am."

"Good boy. Now, take off all your clothes."

Without hesitation the sailor quickly strips off all his clothes and tosses them to the floor.

"You must keep your eyes closed. No matter what, do not open your eyes."

"Yes, ma'am."

"Are you ready for your wax job?"

"Yes, ma'am."

The woman reaches into the closet behind her and retrieves two smooth pieces of wood. She gently places a piece of the smooth wood on each side of his "little sailor."

"Are you sure you're ready for your wax job?"

Eyes still closed, the sailor eagerly replies, "Oh yes, ma'am."

In response, the woman spreads her arms wide and then quickly and forcefully slaps the two pieces of wood back down on each side of his little sailor.

Whack!

And the wax… shot out of his ears.

Sadly, this joke, delivered with great enthusiasm, perfect timing, and spot-on physical gesturing, did not win me the open mic comic contest on the 2012 family Caribbean cruise. I lost out to this:

How can you tell the difference between an oral and a rectal thermometer?

Taste.

Yes, I'm still bitter.

Birth of a Reluctant Tree Hugger

I AM NOT A TREE HUGGER. Don't get me wrong, I do care about the environment. It troubles me that the ozone is disappearing at an alarming rate and that my home state of Florida seems to be destined for shore-to-shore flooding sometime in the not-so-distant future. I recycle and I worry about the polar bears and I believe global warming is real. It's just that on my top ten list of things to worry about, I've got a pecking order that includes equal rights, genocide, world hunger, and panty lines. OK, that last one may not be top-ten worthy, but a gal can only take on so many causes.

However, I also hate to lose. I hate to be bullied. I hate to be wronged. The stubborn Irish in me raises my hackles to a fever pitch when I perceive the underdog is being stepped upon. There was a time when these worlds collided and I found myself right there next to the environmentalists and the hippies and the community organizers, desperately trying to take on big government, big development, and big politics.

In 1999, I had lived in my Springfield townhouse for a little more than two years. As a single, working mom, this home was the first large purchase I had made in my adult life all by my lonesome. Finding a home in a wonderful working-class neighborhood with good schools and lots of kids was a dream come true. This abode was my personal symbol that I could indeed do "it" all by myself. I could work full-time, raise my son, date, save money, pay off student loans (and a car), and buy a home for me and Jimmy. Can you tell I was a little bit proud of myself? I spent many weekends pouring my pride into that townhouse by painting and decorating and putting up wallpaper and falling in love with the place.

When I bought the townhouse, I knew we would be living in the distant shadow of the infamous "mixing bowl" project. The construction was not directly on top of us, but the daily comings and goings of a multi-year, multi-agency, multi-million dollar undertaking less than two miles away couldn't be ignored.

Northern Virginia (NOVA) is infamous for its traffic problems and congestion due to too many people hustling to move about with too few roads. It doesn't help that hundreds of thousands move back and forth between NOVA and DC every day, clogging the two main arteries—I-66 and I-395. In addition, I-495 circles DC and intersects both I-66 and I-395 where large bottlenecks often form. Along these paths, there is a crossroads in Springfield that is the Bermuda Triangle of interstate interchanges. Three of them (I-395, I-95 and I-495) intersect at the location in Springfield where Franconia Road and Old Keene Mill also connect. It had evolved into a giant car-eating mess that half a million drivers attempted to navigate each day, and was not so fondly referred to as the mixing bowl.

In March of 1999 the Virginia Department of Transportation (VDOT) began its eight-year, seven-phase reconstruction of the mixing bowl. The project would become one of the largest highway construction undertakings ever, costing an estimated $676 million. Federal, state, and local governments came together in hopes of developing a permanent solution to one of the largest and most vexing traffic quagmires in the country.

What, you may ask, does all of this have to do with a single working mother and her little ol' 1,200-square-foot townhouse?

Excellent question.

I left the house on an early August morning ready to take on another average day. I dropped Jimmy off at summer camp, caught the blue line metro train out of Springfield, and headed into DC. I don't recall there being anything particularly extraordinary about the day. Because it was August, my day at the Department of Justice (DOJ) was most likely spent reviewing grant proposals for the states, coupled with attending meetings and staying inside because August in DC is a swelter fest.

Returning home that evening, as Jimmy and I turned into the community parking lot and slowly drove closer to our house, we noticed several neighbors walking between the buildings, out toward the back side of our development. There was enough activity to know something was going on. Maybe the kids were having an ad hoc game of hide and seek or kick ball? The neighborhood children often played in the tree grove that separated our small development from a local high school. Since it was nearing dinner time, perhaps the parents were merely rounding up their offspring.

As Jimmy and I got out of the car, I walked over and peered around the corner of the building. Something seemed out of place, the way you look at a room in your house that has been rearranged and it's all the same furniture, but somehow looks off. I soon realized: the trees! All the trees had been cut down.

"What the hell happened?" I asked a parent who I recognized from Jimmy's school and was walking toward me.

"We have no idea. Looks like someone came in today and clear cut the entire oak tree grove."

Fully coming around the back corner of the building, I was greeted by a sea of downed oaks. Strewn haphazardly were at least forty trees, all cut down to stumps. These were not little saplings, they were full grown oak trees which I would discover later were estimated to be at least seventy years old. It was as if someone had clapped his or her hands and—poof!—they all fell down. Massive mounds of branches, limbs and trunks were piled in every direction.

How could this have happened so damn quickly? Looking back toward the townhouse building and my back deck I realized I would now be able to stand in my living room and look straight across what would be barren ground directly on to the high school football field bleachers. I would be privy to a completely unobstructed view of the field—and the lights.

Our Home Owners Association (HOA) president came walking up behind me.

"I heard about this! This is crazy, who would do this?"

"Is this our property?" I asked.

"No, it's an easement that I believe is owned by Fairfax County Schools, but I'm not altogether sure. For all I know this could be the handiwork of some developer."

Jimmy came bolting up to me, took my hand, and asked, "Mom, who killed all these trees?"

"Honey, we have no idea, but we're going to find out."

The next day became a spectacle of errors. Calls to the county Board of Supervisors (BOS), the high school, the school district, and VDOT all resulted in the same answer: We didn't do it. When the contractor arrived early the next morning to begin cleanup, they were asked a simple question:

"Who are you working for?"

The quick answer: "The construction company."

"OK, who is paying your construction company to do this work?"

"Don't know. You'll have to call the office."

This was genuinely messed up.

When the HOA president called me at work to give me an update, I could tell she was beyond frustrated. This was not a woman who ruffled easily.

"I don't know what to do. No one will give me an answer. I have the feeling folks might be scrambling to get their story straight, but, then again, maybe they're counting on this just blowing over. Someone at Fairfax County did suggest that VDOT was paying for the tree removal because of the mixing bowl."

There's a little voice in my head that's supposed to intervene in the event my Irish temper conspires with my Southern sensibilities to right the wrongs of the world. Too many times I've been dragged down the rabbit hole of righteous indignation, only to find myself fighting the good, albeit exhausting, fight. By the age of thirty-five I had some fight left in me, but my days of marches and letter-writing campaigns and demonstrations were dwindling. I had plenty on my plate, thank you very much. However, at this moment, this little voice seemed to have been muzzled—a big, green Irish muzzle.

"The mixing bowl?! What the hell could that work possibly have anything to do with this? That's total BS."

"I agree, but what can we do? What truly burns my butt is that a spokesperson from VDOT attended one of our HOA board meetings over a year ago and assured us the impact on our community would be minimal, maybe a little traffic congestion. Were they lying to us?"

By close of day Friday we were no closer to determining who had authorized the teardown, and weren't being offered any reasonable suggestion as to why the clear-cutting had been necessary. All agreed it was time to bring in the media.

The local press had been itching to report a first-rate screw-up when it came to the mixing bowl project that had been underway for six months. A multimillion-dollar project such as this one was ripe for overpromising, overspending, and overextending its reach. We thought the media might eat this story up. We were right.

We made a few calls, including some big guns like *The Washington Post*, as well as other local papers and TV news stations. Our message: Come see the mess for yourselves. The disaster area behind our complex was still in shambles. They may have been able to fell forty trees in one day, but carving them up, hauling them away and clearing the debris was going to take a lot longer. We pitched the story as government run amok, inept agencies and out of control development with no consideration whatsoever for the environment and our neighborhoods. Mowing over the little people in the name of progress, deforestation killing the planet one community at a time, federal government treading on our land and devaluing our homes. Yep, we hit all the bases. It worked.

By Saturday morning no fewer than four local reporters, including one from *The Post*, and three television news crews descended upon our enclave. One of the parents organized our kids to make protest signs. Nothing plays better for the cameras than cute kids holding signs. Another parent collected signatures from more than 100 homeowners on a petition to request a stop order on the construction until a community meeting could be held. She proudly shared the petition with the press, emphasizing that in the midst of all the mixing bowl commotion our little community mattered.

I soon found myself front and center for the cameras. Our HOA president was not great at public speaking and implored me to be our community spokesperson. I was certainly not the only one working the reporters; many of the community members were being interviewed. However, somehow I was the one who was deemed as the go-to gal for the community. Several hours later there I was on the 11 o'clock news, lamenting the catastrophe next to our community, describing the ridiculous pass-the-buck ineptness we were suffering, and imploring whoever was in charge to stop the process until we could get some answers.

Our initial efforts paid off. Our representative on the county Board of Supervisors (BOS) called to tell us that thanks to our petition he had secured a stop order for the next ten days. It was the best he could do. He highly recommended we call an emergency community meeting and invite every official we could think of to attend.

He also dropped a little bomb that a group of concerned parents from the high school was up in arms. They had been told—by whom it was not clear—that if the construction was halted their kids might not have a baseball field or tennis courts in time for their seasons. Our BOS rep explained he could handle the heat for a little while, but these parents were quickly organizing to make sure the sports careers of their offspring wouldn't be jeopardized. Terrific.

We arranged for a community meeting to take place the following week and the next four days became of whirlwind of phone calls and faxes—this was before the ease of e-mail, I was dealing with dial-up!—and reporter follow-up. Sleeping became a luxury I couldn't afford.

I witnessed a grassroots effort blossom before my eyes. I had never before fully understood that adversity can bring out the very best in people. Neighbors met late into the night, sitting cross-legged on the wooden floor of my living room, discussing strategy and research. We also discussed the crazy rumors that were arising. In the absence of factual information, people tend to make sh*t up. Some of my favorite, though completely inaccurate, rumors included:

* The high school principal was on the take, and had crafted a deal with VDOT to cover the cost of a new baseball field and an administrative building, in return for his willingness to roll over and let the mixing bowl project have three feet of the school's property to put toward a needed on-ramp.

* Cutting down the trees had been a mistake. They were supposed to cut down the trees on the opposite side of the high school.

* The parents of the high school athletes were driving through our neighborhood each night, writing down our car license tag numbers to be targeted on the highways maintained by VDOT. This rumor was particularly paranoia inducing.

* The Governor was going to attend our community meeting. He did not.

* The Secretary of VDOT was going to be fired over this incident. Surprisingly, the VDOT Secretary was fired later in August, but I'll always chalk that one up to coincidence, with maybe a bit of karma mixed in.

When the night of the community meeting arrived, a full blown circus, some of our own making, erupted. Politicians who were running for office asked to address the crowd and promised that under their leadership this kind of travesty of justice would never happen. The parent group from the high school showed up and spread out across three full rows in the back of the room. Our BOS guy provided a very nice opening statement, apologizing for the lack of communication with our neighborhood. VDOT, to its credit, sent a spokesperson who tried to explain it was all a big misunderstanding and only wanted to do what was best for everyone involved. He emphasized that VDOT needed three feet of the high school baseball field in order to build the on-ramp. To do so meant moving the ball field, which in turn meant moving a teacher parking lot, which then led to needing to move the high school tennis courts. There was no option left but to move the courts or the parking lot to the buffer area—property he emphasized was owned by Fairfax County—behind our community that had once been covered in trees. When asked questions about community notification, required public hearings, environmental impact studies, and alternative use of parkland on the other side of the high school, the VDOT sacrificial lamb dodged and ducked and noted more than once "we'll have to get back to you on that."

And then, it was over. The cameras went away, the press lost interest, the furor died down and our ten day stay-of-construction ended. At the one follow-up meeting we were afforded, the VDOT rep snidely noted that I had no idea how close our community had come to having a parking lot in our back yard instead of tennis courts, and perhaps we should count our blessings. Other government officials merely responded by shaking their heads affirmatively and giving me the condescending looks one gives to the crazy cat lady when she's ranting about the aliens coming to steal all her pets. It was a true low point and I've never felt so utterly powerless. The tennis courts were built and our little community learned to live with the additional bit of noise. That year I even received a tennis racket from Santa for Christmas. Yes, apparently St. Nick has a sense of humor.

If there is one bit of silver lining to this story, it's that the experience also provided me a bit of a wake-up call. Being on the other side of the government machine gave me new perspective regarding how I might be perceived when I traveled into communities as a U.S. Department of Justice official. Holy cow, did people in state and local government think I was an A-hole?! Did they believe I was there to lie, to cover-up, and to screw them over? Nothing could have been farther from the truth, but I could now see why people so distrusted the government.

As I was caught up in the drama of the tree-hugging saga, I lost focus of the fact that most people who work within and for the government do so because they want to make a difference. It can be very easy to vilify the great government enemy as some sort of living, breathing, evil entity. The reality is that government is comprised of people who are trying to educate our children, protect our citizens, and clean our streets and waterways. I hope after the great tree takedown and its aftermath I became a better Fed. I also hope that during my days as a Fed I represented government graciously and with an insight that I was there to serve citizens, not myself and not my boss. Yes, I know how hokey that all sounds. Life lessons can sometimes be a little corny.

There's a Leak in the Basement

TODAY, AS I WALKED through a local mall, I heard the sound of a newborn's cry. In the sitting area next to the center atrium Starbucks sat a new mom working diligently to calm her young offspring. Echoing up and out into the surrounding area was the distinctive, high-pitched holler of a hungry baby. Even after all these years—almost twenty-five since I was a new mom—I can still distinguish between hunger, pain, and over-tired infant cries. It's an odd talent that every mom acquires, this ability to assess the needs of a tiny human being based solely upon the tone of his or her wails.

I also can still recall the effect the hunger cry had on my newly minted post-pregnancy mom body. The simple sound of a baby's cry, any baby's cry, could generate an immediate flow of mother's milk. This is a phenomenon not covered with enough importance in Lamaze classes. There is great emphasis placed upon encouraging moms-to-be to breastfeed, which I couldn't agree with more. There are numerous documented health benefits for infants who are breastfed. To this day, I miss 3 a.m. feedings; the whole world is quiet and dark and it's you and your child, alone, with this remarkable bonding time. However, there is little warning offered regarding "control" issues.

When my breast milk first came in, it was like trying to control an opened fire hydrant. I vividly remember standing in the shower and a mere passing thought of my son would cause my breasts to go off as if they were responding to a five-alarm fire. For the first six weeks of my son's life I had to wear thick pads in my nursing bras. It was often difficult to avoid the humiliating reality of drenching the front of my shirt if I so much as laid eyes upon a diaper. There were moments when I was a bit concerned I might drown my son. Luckily, eventually, you somehow gain control over the situation.

Going out in public can be a bit of a challenge during the first few months of motherhood. Unless you're willing to live a cloistered existence, you have to plan your days for as many contingencies as possible while your body transitions from baby maker to baby food supplier. Pads and pumps and loose-fitting shirts with scarves and quick-change tops stuffed in your bag become your new must-have wardrobe essentials.

As I sat there in the mall central court area, sipping my Grande Skinny Vanilla Starbucks latte, I watched the new mom maneuver her child into a discreet nursing position. The crying abated and I found myself smiling and feeling somewhat jealous of this woman and the adventures she would be having. I smiled even wider as I also recalled a time when the whole nursing process threw a bit of a curveball at one of my best friends.

Dani's wedding was planned as a wonderfully laid-back occasion. Second weddings can be so different from our firsts. For many I've attended, the second-time-around nuptials seem to be more about the party and the people and a little less about the dress and the cake. Please don't get me wrong, every gal deserves the wedding of her dreams, whatever that vision may be. It's simply that second weddings seem to be a bit more relaxed. For our gal Dani, this was definitely the case. She had planned the wedding to take place in her beautiful backyard, surrounded by the beginnings of the fall show of colors. Tables would be adorned with wildflowers picked that morning. Friends would contribute homemade creations to the reception feast as part of a grand celebration potluck. Mother Nature wouldn't disappoint and would provide clear blue skies with a slight hint of chill in the air. This would be the kind of day that makes people want to move to Virginia and start a winery.

Monica, also known as Monkee and the third in our trio of thick-as-thieves-since-high-school, had given birth to her beautiful daughter only four months prior to Dani's wedding date. There was no way this wedding could happen without Monkee being there with us. This would be Monkee's first foray away from her daughter for any extended period of time since her birth. What's important to note here is that Monkee is a planner. Every trip, outing, and event we have ever undertaken has come with a full itinerary via our master organizer. No gathering is ever complete without Monkee's top-ten list of must-dos, must-sees, and must-not-misses. This is a woman who buys Christmas presents in July, mails your birthday gift two months in advance, and never shops without a plan of attack that would make General Patton weep with joy. I cannot understand how Monkee is not a Virgo.

On the day of Dani's wedding, Monkee, with her propensity for master planning, had laid out all her options. We arrived earlier than most to help with any last-minute arrangements. Unbeknownst to me, while the rest of us were arranging bud vases and placing chairs outside for guests, Monkee was stashing her breast pump and other necessities in the vanity in the upstairs bathroom. She was so stealth no one was the wiser as she came back downstairs and immediately took over the setting up of the bar area.

Guests began to arrive in earnest about thirty minutes before the ceremony was scheduled to begin. The house and backyard were slowly filling with adults and children and a small quartet began to play lovely background music. I stood on the back upper deck, looked down and across the yard and thought: *This is a perfect day. There is nothing that can go wrong*. I watched as friends and family began staking out their chairs for prime spots for nuptials viewing. As I glanced down at my watch I realized the ceremony was supposed to start in about ten minutes.

Turning back around to go inside, I was greeted by a somewhat frantic looking Monkee sprinting up the deck stairs.

"I've got a situation here," Monkee half-whispered. "I need your help."

"What's wrong?"

"I think Dani is in the bathroom upstairs."

"Is she OK?"

"I'm sure she's fine. That's not the problem."

I stared back at Monkee, unsure where to go with this. I could tell from her distraught expression this was not the moment to make any kind of joke.

"What's wrong?"

"I need a bathroom and there doesn't seem to be one available."

"Can you go the neighbor's house next door?"

"Already thought of that. Doesn't look like anyone's home."

"Is the powder room off the kitchen being used?"

"Yep."

"Well, is there perhaps something downstairs in the basement?" I suggested.

"There's a basement?! Show me. Let's go."

I had been christened the captain of Monkee's bathroom scouting expedition.

Maneuvering back through the house, we opened a door off the hallway that led to wooden stairs down into an unfinished basement. When we reached the bottom I was encouraged to see, over on the left side, a small walled-off space toward the back corner that could be a bathroom. Alas, all that was there was a tiny laundry area with a washer and dryer—no toilet or sink.

"Sorry, Monkee, there doesn't seem to be a toilet down here."

"What? I don't need a toilet."

"Huh? Then what the hell DO you need?"

Monkee's cheeks blushed a bright crimson color as she hesitantly, again in a whisper, said,

"I need some place where I can express some breast milk. I don't understand why this is happening, I took care of this before we left the hotel! But I need to take care of this again and my breast pump is in the upstairs bathroom!"

I couldn't help myself. I grinned.

"This isn't friggin funny Kimba! The wedding is supposed to start…" we both looked down at our watches, "…*now*, the wedding is supposed to start *now*! If I go up there I'm going to soak right through this dress. Dammit!"

Monkee's whisper had quickly turned into a desperate plea for help.

"It feels like I'm already starting to spring a leak here and I don't have an extra dress with me. Do you know how difficult it was to find a suitable dress for this little milk-making factory I'm sporting? What am I going to do?!"

"Sorry, sorry I'm being a jerk. It's going to be OK, we'll can figure something out," I said as I peered around, looking for what I had no idea. Then, I spied something that made me grin again, this time even wider.

"Monkee, I have an idea…."

I walked over toward the corner of the room and pointed down toward the floor.

"How about this?"

"How about what?" replied Monkee.

"How about you use the kitty litter box?"

"The what?! Are you nuts? Kimba, I can't do that."

"Darlin', I don't think you have a lot of options. I'll guard the stairs to make sure no one comes down, there are no windows over on this side of the basement. …I think this is what you're gonna have to do."

Words will never adequately describe the look of panicked horror as Monkee realized this was truly her only viable option. Without saying another word she brushed past me and I walked toward the bottom of the stairs to assume my sentry position.

By now, a full crowd had gathered in the back yard and the quartet was playing a lovely and entertaining tune. And yet, above the buzzing sounds of the gathered wedding attendees, I could soon hear the sounds of Monkee's breast milk hitting the top of the kitty litter.

I couldn't help myself. For the record I am at times an awful person and this was one of those times. I turned around to see the

backside of Monkee bent over from the waist, dress undone, nursing bra unhooked, clearly expressing into the kitty litter box.

"Hey, Monkee, don't forget to write your initials," I blurted out
with a laugh.

"Dammit, I swear I will kill you in your sleep if you do not turn
back around right now and guard those stairs!"

Yes, ma'am. Sorry," I replied as I sheepishly turned back around
to face the stairs and stifle a giggle.

Monkee finished much faster than I had expected and before I
knew it she was back beside me at the bottom of the basement stairs.
She had all the pieces and parts tucked back into place and though
she was still a bit flushed with embarrassment, she looked as beautiful as ever.

Looking me squarely in the eye, and without a hint of humor,
Monkee pronounced, "OK, this is one of those life moments when
you need to swear to me that you are never going to tell anyone
about this... EVER."

"Oh, absolutely. Lips are sealed, promise," I replied.

"Good, now let's get back up there and watch our best friend
get married."

Calmly walking back upstairs and out into the back yard, we
realized we had not missed anything. We turned just in time to see
Dani emerging from the house wearing a beautiful and elegant,
sleeveless, long, white sheath dress. She was, as all brides should
be, radiating pure joy. I looked over at Monkee and winked as I saw
her begin to tear up.

To be fair, I had always meant to keep my secret. I had no plans
to ever even tell Dani of what had transpired in her basement only
minutes before her wedding. As the reception was dwindling down,
and many of the guests had departed, Dani, Monkee and I found
ourselves out on that upper-level deck. This was a rare occurrence
that day when it was only the three of us squirreled away for a brief
moment. Before I knew it, Monkee was gleefully regaling Dani
with a fabulous rendition of how she had utilized the basement as
a makeshift expressing station. At the moment when the three of us

were laughing our hardest, Dani's mom unexpectedly stepped onto the deck and snapped a candid picture. This photo, preserved in an antique wooden frame and perched on my desk for the past twenty years, is by far one of my most cherished possessions. It represents so much of what is fun and happy and silly in my life.

Just so you know, Monkee gave me permission to share this story. I do love a good tale, but I also respect a promise. A great big thank you to all my gal pals who allow me to share our adventures, even the ones that involve a unique way to utilize kitty litter. Do you think the cat ever noticed? Come to think of it, knowing Monkee, she *did* write her initials.

Nutter House

IT'S A DIFFICULT THING to believe, that a poor kid from South Florida could grow up to own a lake house. Second houses are for rich people, right? Homes on the water are for other people, *those* people — people of privilege, wearing all white and lifting sparkling glasses of champagne, toasting to some recent corporate merger.

Well, or so I once thought.

Growing up in Florida, we called them *snowbirds*. They invaded our sunny little state each January and took over our highways, crowded our grocery stores, and occupied our shopping malls. Many were retirees looking for refuge from Old Man Winter. There was also a subset species we called the *shiny birds* — the uber-rich who lived in Palm Beach and came to winter in my home state each year during the *season*. The shiny birds in particular were not of my world. I would read in the newspapers about their cotillions and their masquerade balls and their charity golf tournaments. A mere few miles away, over the intra-coastal bridges, was the domain of the wealthy and the idle rich. These were my skewed childhood impressions of people who owned vacation homes.

I tell you all of this because I'd like you to understand my mindset when, four years ago as our son was graduating from high school and venturing on to college, my husband started to broach the "what's next" and "what if" conversations with me. With Jimmy moving on, where did we see ourselves in five to ten years? My response: We would be right here in Fairfax, saving for retirement, right?

Gingerly, hubby began to slip into conversations casual mentions of weekends spent fishing or boating or sunning on a dock somewhere. Perhaps we should venture further out into Virginia and Maryland? Go see the sites, drive along the coast, and spread our wings a bit. He was oh so crafty. Shelter magazines (my absolute addiction) began to appear on the dining table with images of beautiful coastal escapes on their picturesque covers. Oh, he knows me so well. I became hooked the minute I started envisioning imaginary vacation home decorating.

Thus our house-hunting adventures began, the idea being we would take our time and explore our options without any need to commit to property purchasing in the foreseeable future. On weekends we traveled the eastern shores of Maryland, and the beaches of the Chesapeake Bay, and the mountainous western part of Virginia. Nothing was off-limits. We considered cabins and shacks, beachfront and lakeside; large, open floor plans with expansive views, as well as cozy bungalows with quirky character. We toured many wonderful homes, but we weren't swept off our feet. I needed to fall in love, to be struck by lightning, to find a home I couldn't stop thinking about.

Then, three years ago, we discovered *Nutter House*.

We didn't always call it *Nutter House*. Initially, it was simply the big-windows house on Virginia's Smith Mountain Lake with these incredible breath-taking views. It offered everything we were looking for, and then some. I found myself coming back to this big-windows house in my mind's eye. Wouldn't a favorite steamer trunk in our basement look lovely situated in the corner of that sun room? My vintage robin's-egg-blue Pyrex dishes would be perfect in the all-white kitchen. A shabby chic table I had spied on deep discount would look wonderful in the dining area.

Not surprisingly, although it was the perfect house and I had in fact fallen in love, I had trouble agreeing to a purchase offer.

Window shopping is one thing, actually buying property—that is a completely different kettle of fish. The agent we were working with (who would later become one of my dearest and steadfast gal pals at the lake) was blessedly patient because we should have been willing to commit to the big-windows house immediately. My hesitation was buried deep in my Florida past. Spending money and taking on debt was a gigantic and almost insurmountable obstacle. Vacation homes, second homes, only existed in the world of the snowbirds. Like a man trying to summon the courage to propose, I found myself nervously stalling and looking for excuses to avoid commitment. Tragically, it took a shout-out from the cosmos to push me through my roadblock.

Three years ago, as I was preparing for a radio interview, I looked up as my husband walked into the room, his pale face stunned and frozen. He possessed an expression of such significant and utter disbelief that I knew immediately something was terribly wrong. Taking in a sharp breath, my husband looked at me and said two words I will never forget:

"Greg's gone."

"Greg? Greg who?"

"Greg Johnson. He's gone."

Greg was my husband's best friend—his best friend since he was fourteen years old. When he had said "Greg" I couldn't fathom he had meant Greg Johnson. Greg Johnson couldn't be gone. Greg was the same age as my husband. Greg had been at our house the week prior, helping us repair some electrical problems. How could he be *gone*?

Yet, in the blink of an eye, Greg had left this world. It was a brutal wake-up call. During the week leading up to the funeral, I found myself pondering the giving and receiving of emotional comfort. At the times when we need it most, how do we support and care for each other? What comforts do we seek?

For many of us, foods and the memories associated with those foods often bring comfort. My own oddball comfort foods include:

Potato salad with no eggs (because that's how Mom always makes it special for me);

Barbecued Fritos (because I only allow myself to indulge when I'm really down or on a road trip); and,

Salmon loaf, which was one of my grandmother's favorite things to make (even if most of the family didn't like it).

There is also one especially comforting symbol that seems to manifest in my life at just the right moments: the bicentennial quarter.

My Grumps left this world in June 1976. He barely missed the two-hundredth celebration of our country's independence. I'm not sure exactly when, but somewhere along my path I started to collect bicentennial quarters because they always remind me of Grumps and what a wonderful, loving presence he was in my life. These quarters have become increasingly scarce as the years have gone by; finding one now is always a surprise and comfort.

You may be asking yourself: what does any of this have to do with buying a lake house? I promise you there is a deep and profound connection between Greg's death, bicentennial quarters, and *Nutter House*.

Right before Greg's funeral a group of friends and family were helping prepare the family home for visitors. I watched my husband cope by quickly snapping into recovery mode as he focused his energies on supporting Greg's wife, young daughter and other family members. As the work progressed, I volunteered to make a lunch run for sandwiches and sodas. I placed the order and as I patiently waited my mind wandered over the sadness of losing such a special person. As I absent-mindedly paid for the sandwiches, there in the change being handed to me across the counter was a worn bicentennial quarter. It had been at least a year since I had seen one in circulation. In that unforeseen moment, as I stared at the cashier's outstretched hand, I was comforted by this tiny sign.

After some time had passed and the reality of Greg's death had begun to set in, I shared with my husband how Grumps had found a way to comfort me. I hoped somehow my husband could find a way to allow me to comfort him, too. He sat there across from me, eyes down, and when he looked up he said,

"Let's not wait until it's too late. Let's buy the big-windows house." Without hesitation, I agreed.

Four months later, we closed on the big-windows house at Smith Mountain Lake. It was one of the best decisions we've ever made. Each weekend we visit the lake, each early morning when I look out over the water, I'm sure both Grumps and Greg are smiling down on us.

How did it become *Nutter House?* One day, I was chatting with Jane, our real estate agent extraordinaire turned gal pal, and sharing that I was obsessed with giving the house a name. All those rich people I had watched while growing up had always given their yachts and houses such fun monikers. Now that I was officially one of *those* people, didn't I need to give my home a name? Jane smiled and shared that when her son was young, he would ask her,

"Did you sell another house today, Mom?"

She would reply,

"Yep, they up and bought *a nutter* house."

At the very moment Jane shared this story, I reached into my coat pocket—a coat I had not worn for several months—and found that bicentennial quarter I had received in the change for those sandwiches. I smiled and knew we had our home name: *Nutter House.* The quarter is safely tucked away in a *Nutter House* nook—a little charm to keep all those who enter safe and happy.

Our comforts may come to us in unexpected ways—a bag of Fritos, some homemade potato salad, or a small worn quarter. I do believe the universe speaks to us often, if we pay attention and listen. If you're ever in the Smith Mountain Lake area, and you find yourself needing to borrow a quarter, please do stop by. I'll probably be around back, on the dock, wearing a funny hat and happily running my mouth. Well, what did you expect from someone who lives in a place called *Nutter House?*

*   *   *

This essay is included in "Voices from Smith Mountain Lake," an anthology published October 2013 by the Smith Mountain Arts Council.

Why the World Needs Virgos

VIRGO
August 23 – September 22
Earth Sign, Ruled By Mercury
Mission: *Completing the World's To-Do List One Task at a Time*
Motto: *Step Up, Take Charge, Move On*

I WISH I COULD BE MORE like my dog. Even at thirteen years old, Taz greets each day as if he's never traveled out along our curvy neighborhood sidewalks. He eagerly runs in circles by the front door, awaiting our venture outside. Unlike Taz, I need to slowly roll into the daylight. On morning walks you'll find me consuming strong black coffee from a battered travel mug as Taz's long red mesh leash tugs me along. Most mornings are peacefully uneventful. However, sometimes The Fates throw you a curve.

One recent morning as we ambled down the main thoroughfare of our community I spied our local school bus stopped and blocking traffic in the middle of our neighborhood intersection. We don't live in an extraordinarily traffic-heavy area, but at 8 a.m. many neighbors are heading out to work and our little crossroads can quickly becoming congested. Parents milled about and kids, full of new-day energy just like Taz, playfully ran around on both sides of the street. All seemed quite oblivious to the large yellow object straddled across the intersection.

Curiosity getting the best of me, Taz and I walked up and I called out to the nearest adult,

"What's going on?"

Several parents turned to look at me and then to each other with expressions akin to having been asked to solve the mystery of Stonehenge. Absolutely no response was provided. Was this none of my business or some weird shun-the-non-school-age-parent moment?

Troubled, and because I will never learn to stay out of such things, I pulled Taz next to me and strode into the intersection. Leaning in and peering up through the open door of the school bus, I cautiously asked the driver,

"Hey, you OK? Bus broken down?"

"Nope," replied Mr. Bus Driver. "I'm early and I can't leave until 8:15 a.m."

This reply from the driver was delivered in a surprisingly matter-of-fact manner, and conveyed his judgement that blocking an intersection in the middle of morning traffic was wholly reasonable and within all expectations of a school bus driver.

"Hmm, well, you're kind of blocking traffic. Folks won't drive around you because you're driving a school bus, so, could you pull over?"

"Why sure, thanks, I'll do that," he cheerfully replied, seemingly unaware of the congestion his immobile bus was causing.

After a bit of maneuvering, the bus was safely situated along the side of the road. Unfortunately, cars continued to back up in all directions, as apprehensive drivers remained hesitant to pass through an intersection teeming with children.

Did any other adult offer assistance? Nada. Not a single one. They all seemed completely unaware of the situation, intently carrying on conversations or sitting in their parked minivans, busily scrolling through their smart phone apps and Facebook pages. I soon found myself juggling leash, tugging dog, and blue plastic poop bag precariously with my right hand, my coffee mug in the left, and directing traffic through the intersection while simultaneously shooing children out of the road. As cars passed precariously close, a few drivers honked in appreciation; one even offered to take the bag of poop off my hands. That was a kind soul indeed. The bus driver also offered a robust wave goodbye as he drove off with the neighborhood offspring at exactly 8:15 a.m. Many of the kids were waving at, I suspect, Taz.

In case there was any doubt, this, my friends, is why the world needs Virgos. You're welcome.

REFLECTIONS FROM THE MIDDLE-AGED CHEAP SEATS

There once was a gal quite regaled,
For telling her crazy-ass tales.
Her book makes you laugh,
Describing her gaffes.
Now just $2.99—what a sale!

—Kim Dalferes, *The Middle-Aged Cheap Seats*

NO ONE IS MORE SURPRISED than me that I've become a blogger. I started *The Middle-Aged Cheap Seats* because I was told I *must* write a blog. The only way readers were going to find me, and by extension my books, was through the Internet. I needed a platform, an Internet presence. Ugh, right?

When I began this journey, I had NO idea what to expect. Would I be able to find something interesting to write about on a regular basis? Would anyone stop by, read, and maybe leave a comment? Would the blog become a giant time-suck and get in the way of my job, writing, marriage, and growing fondness for naptime (not necessarily in that order)?

I made a one-year commitment, and based in part on a few *aha* moments along the way, I continue to blog my heart out more than three years later. My blog also picked up a title: "The Middle-Aged Cheap Seats." Not at all sure how that happened, but it seems to fit.

Some of my favorite revelations have been:

I don't blog very often about my books, even if I do weave in my writing every now and then (see how I did that?).

I've been able to find something interesting to write about each month. And, blogging has become something I look forward to; it's not a chore.

Illustrations, top ten lists, and quick references resonate with readers.

I don't have to be brilliant in all my posts, but my goal should always be to create content that is colorful, easy to read, and provides a little value and sometimes a giggle.

Blogging has connected me with some wonderful groups and resources, including *The Women of Facebook, Midlife Boulevard, Better After 50,* and *Celebrating Authors.* I highly recommend you check out all these groups. I hope you'll visit them—please tell 'em Kimba sent you.

What follows are some of my favorite posts. Some have been expanded a bit because I almost always have a little bit more I would like to say.

Time Travel: What I Would Tell 18-Year-Old Kimba

I WAS RECENTLY HAVING lunch with a friend and we were discussing her current work as a college professor. She asked why I hadn't gone back to the college classroom. Yep, I was once an adjunct professor. I know—shocking! I lamented that I loved teaching, but I haven't had the time to return to campus. To be frank, it would take quite a bit of effort to get up to speed on everything that has developed in criminology over the past two decades. That seems like a lot of work and I'm not as ambitious as I used to be.

This also got us to talking about how much things in general have changed since I was a college freshman over three decades ago. When you start to reflect back, the view from the middle-aged cheap seats sure is fascinating. To quote the wise and lyrical Rod Stewart: *I wish that I knew what I know now, when I was younger.* If I could go back in time and have a conversation with my former 18-year-old self, there are a few things I would want to say:

1. **Don't worry about the money**. Money issues tend to work themselves out. You can continue to be frugal, just like your Nana, but don't let worrying about finances define you as a person.

2. **Your kid brother is a great guy**. At eighteen you think he is a pain in the ass. At fifty you think he is a wonderful soul.

3. **Start using moisturizer.** IMMEDIATELY. Come to think of it, make it a moisturizer with sun block, at least SPF 30. I am not kidding.

4. **Wait for lightning to strike.** It's a bit difficult to believe at eighteen, but some day you will be struck by lightning (figuratively speaking). Someone will rock your world and make you go weak in the knees, and you will understand what all the fuss is about. Don't settle for anything less than being swept full force off your feet; it's worth the wait.

5. **Love FSU.** Florida State may not be your first choice for the school you want to attend, but you are going to become one of its biggest fans and you will absolutely fall in love with FSU. GO NOLES!

6. **Your life will not turn out as expected**. You won't be a lawyer. I know you're a Virgo and you're going to obsessively plan. Doesn't matter—when you least expect it life is going to take a few surprising turns. That's just the way it works. Try to trust in the universe.

7. **Don't listen to unnecessary criticism**. A freshman English professor is going to tell you that you have no writing talent. She is an idiot and thirty years later you won't even remember her name.

8. **In ten years, invest in something called the "Internet."** Trust me.

9. **Be more adventurous**. That offer for those free backstage passes to the Prince concert, the ones you are going to turn down because you have to study: TAKE THEM. Prince is going to be huge.

10. **Wear a better bra.** Some day you are going to regret that lack of support.

How Do You Know She's a Witch?

We have found a witch, may we burn her?
How do you know she is a witch?
She looks like one!

—*Monty Python and the Holy Grail*

HMM… WHAT EXACTLY does a witch look like?

The sad truth is that by most estimates, up through the 1700s, 40,000 or more people worldwide were executed under suspicion of practicing witchcraft, based primarily upon their religious beliefs, independent or rebellious behaviors, and some interesting physical characteristics including… **left-handedness**.

Being a southpaw myself, I've always been somewhat fascinated by societal views of left-handedness. However, it was not until I read a recent news article that I came to understand that left-handers have been feared and persecuted for thousands of years.

In the English language, the term *left* is derived from the Anglo-Saxon *lyft* meaning to be weak or broken. This aversion to all things lefty is not limited to only the English language: The German for "left-handed' is *linkisch*, which means awkward, clumsy, and maladroit. In Italian, *mancino* is derived from crooked or maimed. In Russian, to be called a left-hander—*levja*—is a term of insult. Sheesh!

It's a wonder left-handedness hasn't been wiped out. After all, only ten percent of the population is left-handed. Scholars note it appears we've held steady at this percentage for about 30,000 years. Despite the persecution, the fear (left-handedness having once been considered the mark of the devil), and a propensity to be accident prone, we've survived. There are a few theories as to why this is true:

It's genetic. One premise is that the gene LRRTM1 is a strong contributing factor for left-handedness. Scientists discovered the gene during a study of dyslexic children. It's believed this particular irregularity is inherited from the father. At the most, this seems to account for twenty-five percent of all lefties. In my family, the only other lefty I've ever been able to identify is my Uncle Tommy, on my mama's side, so go figure.

It's the environment. There might be conditions during pregnancy that contribute to developing into a left-hander. Here is my favorite: Left-handers were originally in the womb with a twin who did not survive, or a "vanishing twin." Two of me? I do not think my mother would have survived two teenage Kimbas.

It's a choice. For whatever reason, some infants may simply choose to be lefties. Are we more rebellious? Are we stubborn? Do we choose to be left-handed because we are more creative? I find this one particularly funny because I can tell you: I was born a lefty. I've never been able to do anything right-handed. For me, it would be like trying to choose my eye color or my height or my shoe size. My GeeGee tried desperately to teach me to knit. I remember clearly the day she exclaimed, quite exasperated, "Kim, you're just going to have to choose to knit right-handed." My response: "No Grandma, you're gonna have to choose to teach me left-handed." To this day "knit one, purl two" is lost on me.

It's not all gloom, doom, and bad luck for us lefties, though I admit it's hard to ignore sayings like this Scottish one: *He's so unlucky, he must have been baptized by a left-handed priest.* There have, in fact, been quite a few famous and successful left-handers, including: scientists—Albert Einstein, Benjamin Franklin, and Marie Curie; presidents—four of the past seven (Ford, Bush Sr., Clinton, and Obama); and actors—Cary Grant, Marilyn Monroe, and, a personal favorite, Hugh Jackman.

The truth is, I like possessing distinctive qualities. I like being tall, big-footed, green-eyed and, yes, left-handed. To celebrate our uniqueness, we even have our own day: August 13th is International Left-Handers Day (I'm guessing unlucky thirteen must have been chosen on purpose here). I'm happy to represent ten percent of the population. And have you noticed I haven't exactly denied the whole witch thing?

In Search of: Angry White Male

HERE IN VIRGINIA we are once again in the middle of the silly season commonly known as an election year. Are you weary? I know I am. Is it me, or does all the rancor seem to be a giant non-stop loop of visceral bickering and name-calling? Just last year a somewhat shocking and nasty encounter right after the national election prompted me to pen this open letter to Angry White Male (AWM). It could, unfortunately, easily apply to this year as well.

Dear AWM,

Let me start by noting I understand how disappointed you are that your candidate did not win the race to become President of the United States. I've been on the losing side of an election and I know it can make you feel awfully dejected. No one likes to lose, especially an election where so much rhetoric was produced by heated debates and with no clear front runner going right up to Election Day. I honestly do understand your passion and commitment to a candidate and a cause. What I do not understand is hatred based solely upon a bumper sticker.

When you walked across the grocery store parking lot, and began screaming at me "THANK YOU FOR DESTROYING MY

COUNTRY!!" I at first thought you must have been yelling at someone else. Why on earth would a stranger, someone I had never laid eyes on before in my life, be screaming at me at 9 a.m.?! It took a few seconds for my not-yet-awake-brain to register you were actually yelling at ME... because of the bumper sticker on my car. I did try to be rational: I emphasized I didn't even know you. Your repeated screaming of "THANK YOU FOR DESTROYING MY COUNTRY!!!" caused me to regrettably lose my cool and digress to calling you a not-so-nice slang term for the body part used to sit on a chair. I sincerely wish I had not done that.

What I wish I had done instead was invite you to walk across the parking lot to the local Starbucks and have a cup a coffee with me. Why? Because there a few things I would like to tell you about me and why I truly love my country:

– I believe in democracy and I believe in the process, even if I don't always like the outcome. Our political system has endured and flourished for more than two centuries. We are so fortunate to live in a place where both you and I can vote and choose our leaders. I do not take this for granted.

– I am the wife of a veteran. I've lived through a long deployment and every day I'm proud my family has been able to serve our country in this way.

– I've worked my entire career—as a state and federal government employee as well as within the non-profit arena—to improve the lives of adults, protect children, and keep our communities safe. I chose this career because I wanted to make our country a better place, not because I ever wanted to destroy it. I am not the enemy; I am your neighbor.

So much of what is wrong with our nation right now is per-petuated by this "if you do not agree with me you are the enemy" mentality. Americans need to be better than this. A recent article by *the always-brilliant Danielle Brian of the Project on Government Oversight noted: "All this anger and unwillingness to listen, currently typical of the American public, is also typical in Congress. Gridlock and paralysis are the new norm as the members of Congress stick blindly to their party lines, rather than acting in the best interest of our nation." My position is that we cannot expect members of Congress to behave better if we don't start with the person in the mirror.*

So, AWM, I hope your anger subsides. I hope you will never again accost a stranger in a parking lot based on nothing more than a sticker on a car bumper. I believe you are better than that. I bet your Mama raised you better than that.

Sincerely,
Proud Non-Destroyer of this Country

Bar Fight

IT LOOKED TO BE NOTHING. A pimple no bigger than a sesame seed, which would get a little scaly, flake off, and go away, only to return a few weeks later. Over many months I went through this little cycle often, each time thinking, *hmmm... I wonder if I should get this looked at?*

One day, instead of flaking away, the little spot started to bleed. We're not talking something akin to a zombie flick here, just a little irritated area. When I showed my spot to Dad this past July, he noted, "Ya know, kiddo, you should go have that checked." No sugar-coating from Dad; the very nudge I needed.

Skin cancer is prevalent in my family. Irish ancestry and Florida sunshine do not mix well. What I was honestly prepared for was a quick little, *We can take care of this right here in the office, no big deal.*

What I was a little surprised to hear from my dermatologist was, "I believe we should take a biopsy."

What I was incredibly surprised by was the diagnosis: basal cell carcinoma. Skin cancer.

Let's go over a few terms, because everyone out there needs to be educated:

Basal Cell Carcinoma (BCC). BCC is the most common form of skin cancer. Nearly three million cases are diagnosed each year. In almost all cases it is *not* life threatening. According to the U.S. National Library of Medicine, the risk factors for BCC include:

1. Light-colored or freckled skin

2. Blue, green, or gray eyes

3. Blond or red hair

4. Overexposure to x-rays or other forms of radiation

5. Many moles

6. Close relatives who have or had skin cancer

7. Many severe sunburns early in life

8. Long-term daily sun exposure

Would you believe I met seven out of eight of these factors? Hello?!

Melanoma. This is the most serious form of skin cancer. This was *not* my diagnosis and I am forever grateful.

Mohs Procedure. With my diagnosis, my dermatologist referred me for a Mohs procedure. Dr. Frederick Mohs developed this surgical procedure, which is considered to be the most effective way to treat skin cancer. This type of surgery removes the least amount of tissue while at the same time ensuring clean margins—clean meaning the area is deemed cancer-free. The success rate for Mohs procedures is nearly ninety-nine percent. You can see why I like my odds here.

You may ask yourself, why am I sharing all this? Because knowledge is power. I was lucky to have a good friend who had experience with skin cancer and talked me through what I could expect during and after the surgery. Even with this wonderful source of support and information, I was still a bit unprepared for the extent of the procedure. That small, scaly imperfection was hiding a bigger problem right below the surface.

Here's what I want to emphasize: If you're wondering about *anything*, go get it checked out. This one-inch scar I'll be sporting will fade, but will remain my little reminder to always make my health a priority.

Please know I'm working to keep matters in perspective. I do not for one minute regard skin cancer as a laughing matter. However, there are many, many illnesses and afflictions far more serious. I'm committed to a healthy awareness of the risks of skin cancer, but wish to keep my circumstances grounded and proportional. I do understand and appreciate that I am extraordinarily lucky.

I'm now on a quest to create some background. This newly acquired facial scar of mine needs a good story. My current favorite is that I got it in a bar fight with a University of Florida cheerleader. I'm also considering tales that include a foot-in-mouth incident, a close encounter with an iguana, or perhaps something involving kissing George Clooney. If you have other suggestions, please send them my way.

Finally, a little shout-out to the wonderful doctors and staff at the Skin Cancer Surgery Center of Fairfax, Virginia. Your exemplary care and support are most definitely appreciated.

Dog Wisdom

THIS PAST MONTH one of my best friends left this world. Our dog, Taz, the little miracle mutt who survived a crazy emergency surgery last year, finally succumbed to old age at thirteen. Up until quite recently, he was still chasing squirrels and had hauled ass after a fox that appeared in the flower bed. For most of his life Taz was a happy, healthy mutt from the pound whom we loved dearly. I sure do miss him.

For those of you who have read my first book, *I Was In Love With a Short Man Once*, you understand my relationship with Taz was not always one of full love and mutual admiration. We survived, sometimes barely, incidences of peeing on the Christmas tree and eating the smoked salmon off the kitchen counter. It took me quite a while to fully recover from the "ate my wedding bouquet" incident.

Over time I came to love and appreciate life with Taz, even the puppy mishaps and the stubborn "I'm not going out in the snow" tugs-of-war. The universe does not always offer advice and motivation through a dramatic burning bush or a spectacular show of nature's power. Sometimes, if you genuinely pay attention, quiet little lessons sneak into your thoughts in the most interesting ways.

Here are a few of my favorite Taz-induced insights, let's call them *Tazisms*:

1. A sad puppy face can get you out of a lot of trouble.

2. A little nap in a sunny spot is a good solution to any problem.

3. You CAN teach an old dog new tricks. We rescued Bonz the cat when Taz was eleven. He rolled with it like they had always cohabitated.

4. Almost everything tastes better with a little smidge of peanut butter on it.

5. No matter how old you get, you still wanna run with the pack every once in a while.

6. A cheerful little wag of your tail often gets you what you want.

7. Love unconditionally; it is contagious.

8. It's rarely fun to be stuck in the doghouse.

9. Just because you mark your territory doesn't mean it's actually yours.

10. You will never regret being someone's very best and most loyal friend.

Rest in peace, dear ol' friend. I hope you're chasing your fill of squirrels and that you've found a sunny place to nap on GeeGee and Grumps' heavenly front porch.

Secrets of an Estate Sale Junkie

"HELLO, MY NAME IS KIM, and I'm an Estate Sale Junkie."

"Hello, Kim!"

I wasn't always an ESJ. I began with what seemed to be relatively harmless excursions: thrift store perusing, perhaps the random yard or garage sale were as far as I explored. It all changed when, about a year ago, Dad introduced me to the intriguing underworld known as the *estate sale network*.

I've come to understand that estate sales are different from the standard garage sale. A garage or yard sale is usually small in scope and tends to include items that folks are merely trying to get rid of—old toys, lots of clothes, maybe the random household item. With an estate sale, the contents of the whole house are up for grabs. Another big difference: Estate sales are almost always organized by professional companies.

Dad got hooked when a friend casually asked him to tag along to a local estate sale. He was fascinated by the yard tools, Pyrex dishes, and Christmas china—all being sold at terrific prices. He was soon calling me weekly to describe his latest "score," and assuring me there was no reason to ever pay retail again.

Last year, during a visit to the West Coast, we accompanied Dad to an estate sale to see what all the fuss was about. We arrived at the first sale a full forty-five minutes before it was scheduled to start. This would be my first glimpse of the ESJ subculture. Feeling a bit like an amateur anthropologist, I observed the tribe with its accepted rules of conduct. A hierarchy was established through the distribution of numbers which dictated where you would be placed in line for admission to the sale. I was surprised to find out the woman who I deemed to be a tribe queen, the woman who disseminated the numbers, was self-appointed! She did not work for the estate sale company that had organized the sale. She simply stepped in and took charge. Fascinating.

Four sales later I began to understand Dad's addiction. It was the thrill of the hunt, the idea that perhaps you'd find something akin to those million-dollar Rhino Cups featured on last year on an episode of the PBS series *Antiques Roadshow*. I was hooked.

Back home, I subscribed to estatesales.net (the best source I've found for estate sale news and events). I began to scour the featured sale photos weekly. I searched for intriguing artifacts worthy of an early morning trip in ridiculous Northern Virginia traffic.

Now, a full year in, I've learned there are a few **ESTATE SALE RULES OF ENGAGEMENT:**

Arrive early and respect the numbering process. I've seen two sweet looking little ol' ladies almost throw down because one was not abiding by her place in line.

Cash is king. Most estate sales only take cash. Read the sale fine print before you arrive.

If you want it, pick it up. Possession is the law. I once picked up a bathroom trashcan which I thought I might buy. Another woman stealthily stalked me throughout the house, hoping I would put it down. I bought the thing on principle. It looks quite nice in my powder room, thank you very much.

Merchandise selection is best on the first day, cheapest on the final day. Most estate sales run Thursday or Friday through Sunday. Thursdays you will get the best selection, but by Sunday what's left will usually be half price.

The best deals are yard tools and kitchen items. For my son's first college apartment we bought almost all the items for his kitchen at estate sales. Yard tools are almost always a good deal, too, but they go fast so walk through the garage first.

Play by the rules. I recently watched a woman go through a sale and mark items with yellow sticky tabs. She noted this meant the items had been sold. I found out later she didn't work for the estate sale company, she was purely being greedy! She had no intention of buying all those items, she only wanted more time to "shop." FOUL! Don't be that girl.

Once you buy it, you own it. Inspect items carefully before you purchase. If it's cracked or chipped make sure you aren't paying too much.

Keep your expectations low. Looking for Pyrex dishes and glass cake plates—you're gonna score. If you think you're going to find a Tiffany lamp for two dollars, you're going to be disappointed.

Watch for "good bones." Most furniture is likely to be either expensive antiques or especially worn out and dated. Be on the lookout for pieces that are sturdy, but may be in need of a little update.

Estate sales aren't for everyone. Husband Greg won't tag along anymore. He feels uncomfortable riffling through the possessions of the recently deceased. But, if you're a bargain hunter and you want to meet some truly interesting people, you just might be a fellow ESJ. One of the best ESJs: Cari Cucksey who hosts *Cash and Cari* on HGTV. I am a huge Cari fan and love her ESJ tips and advice.

Please do let me know when you discover a major treasure. I'll be jealous, but honestly pleased for you.

Never Trust Someone
With Thin Lips

I'M SOMETIMES ASKED "where do you get inspiration for your blog topics?" Most days the blogging gods simply speak to me. Take today, for example: This is my thirteenth blog post, and today is Friday the thirteenth. Coincidence? Hmm…. It appears the question of the day is: "Are you a superstitious person? Do you believe in luck?"

Superstitions, by definition, are beliefs based in something supernatural or a feeling or an instinct. Some superstitions may be somewhat fact-based: It may be bad luck to walk under a ladder because it is, in fact, unsafe to walk under a ladder.

I am most definitely superstitious. In particular, I become ridiculously superstitious when I'm gambling. On a hot craps table, with a hot shooter, I'll leave the table once that shooter is done. When a new blackjack dealer rotates onto the table, if I lose three hands in a row, I'll switch to a different table.

I come from a long line of superstitious Irishmen (and women). My Irish Nana had all kinds of "Nanaisms." Her personal belief system was strong:

Never trust a man with a widow's peak.

Never trust someone with thin lips. (This one is a bit trouble-some for me since, as I get older my lips seem to be thinning out. Am I becoming less trustworthy? Yeah, probably.)

Never wear your hat in the house and never place your hat on the table.

Nana also believed she could get rid of warts by spitting on them. I'm here to tell you, when I was a kid she spit on a wart on my left middle finger and I swear that sucker was gone the next day.

I've always been fascinated with the superstitious underpin-nings of most sports. Baseball in particular seems to have its own magical code of superstitions and good luck traditions. Who hasn't heard of the curse of the Bambino? And a serious heads-up: Never, ever, discuss a no-hitter while it's in progress. A pitcher in the midst of a possible no-hitter, or the even more elusive perfect game, will sit remotely by himself at the end of the dugout bench to avoid any discussion that could jinx his performance.

President Franklin Roosevelt was famously superstitious, suffer-ing from triskaidekaphobia (also known as the fear of the number 13). Today, and this blog, would have troubled him. It has been reported he changed travel dates or the number of people attending a dinner party in order to avoid the dreaded number thirteen.

You may think superstitions and beliefs in luck are a bunch of hooey. Still, can you honestly tell me that if a black cat crossed your path you wouldn't view this as a bad sign? By the way, what do people who own black cats do? Do they freak out every time the cat walks across the room?

I've come across other superstitions that are not as universally well known as the black-cat omen:

Dreaming of a lizard is a sign that you have a secret enemy. OK, someone is gonna have to explain this one to me.

It's bad luck to change the name of a horse or a boat.

It's bad luck to carry a banana on a boat (there are all kinds of theories about the origins of this superstition).

If your palms itch you're going to come into money.

Whatever your beliefs, I wish you luck and good fortune today, and please be careful out there.

Whoa, I Just Said What?!

AS IT'S THE END OF THE YEAR, I've been reflecting a bit on the happenings in my life across the past twelve months. Overall, from my vantage point up here in the middle-aged cheap seats, it was a pretty good year. We did have too many good friends leave this world to move on to their next adventures. Reaching the mid-life marker seems to bring with it the reality that life is indeed short and not to be taken for granted.

This year brought many opportunities for me to do or say things I never thought I would ever, well, do or say. I am somewhat infamous for putting my crazy, Southern, Irish foot in my mouth. It's simply the law of averages: When you talk as much as I do, it's only a matter of time before something comes out wrong. However, this is a little different. These are things I did or said over the past year that were unique to this particular point in my life.

Therefore, following in the footsteps of the great David Letterman, here is Kimba's List of Top Ten Surprising Things She Said This Year:

Number Ten: "Can I get a re-tweet (RT)?"

Number Nine: "Where's the cat?" (spoken by previous member of Team Canine).

Number Eight: "Oh, I see. I'm not pregnant; it's just menopause."

Number Seven: "Damn this small print. Where are my readers?"

Number Six: "I'm OK with the term 'cougar.'"

Number Five: "Yep, just sent off the last tuition payment to Penn State."

Number Four: "Would you take a dollar for this glass measuring cup?" (Uttered at every estate sale in the DC metro area).

Number Three: "I look great… for sixty." (Modified from my previous "I look great… for fifty" mantra.)

Number Two: "Ryan Reynolds may actually be hotter than George Clooney."

And the Number One Most Surprising Thing Kimba Said This Year: "What do I do? Well, I'm a writer."

Mysteries of the Universe

THERE ARE THINGS in the universe I truly don't understand. Actually, I'm keeping a list of the things I don't understand—no surprise here since I'm a Virgo and we Virgos love lists. I have this plan—of course I have a plan, see previous Virgo reference—that when I get to the pearly gates, St. Peter (aka Heaven's Bouncer) is going to ask me, "Do you have any questions before you proceed?"

I'm going to be ready to reply: "Why yes, since you asked…"

Here are some of the secrets of the universe for which I would like an explanation or maybe a little bit of background info:

Why is it that as soon as a gal finds the perfect mascara or bra, it gets discontinued? Am I wrong? Damn you Kiehl's! Your mineral mascara was fabulous.

How can Taco Bell be so bad for you and yet so incredibly delicious?

So, men get aging gracefully and women get childbirth? How is this even remotely fair? My husband looks better now than the day I married him more than a decade ago.

Speaking of men, what's the deal with their obsession over packing the car for vacation? It's called a VA-CA-TION... throw the crap in the way-back and get on the road! OK, boys, hit me with your best shot with your replies to this one, because I'm not sure poor Peter will be able to explain.

While you're at it, guys, care to explain your propensity for leaving wet towels on the floor and dirty dishes in the sink? Women REALLY don't understand this.

What's up with mammogram machines? The universe couldn't inspire someone to create one made out of pillows or something equally soft and comfy? We have inventions like the "Shake Weight" and the "Chia Pet," but no one's improved the process of having our breasts smashed between two cold plastic plates? I do not understand.

What's the universe's beef with the Florida State University baseball program? Over twenty-one appearances at the College World Series and you couldn't let them win even once? Did an FSU player pee in someone's Wheaties or something?

That's all I have for now. I sure hope St. Peter has something akin to Wikipedia at his disposal. Or, maybe he'll simply roll his eyes and wave me through to the Big Guy.

Smells Like Football

WHEN MY SON, JIMMY, was six years old, we were coming home one evening and as we stepped up onto the front stoop and I reached to unlock the front door, he looked up at me and said,

"Mom, there are frogs in those bushes."

"Oh, yeah," I replied. "How do you know?"

"Because I can *smell* them."

His little beaming face conveyed such pure excitement, I do believe he truly could smell those frogs. That kind of glee, that sheer joy of anticipating something exciting that's waiting to be discovered, is how I feel each September at the start of football season.

I love football. I know *loving* something like football seems silly, but I do, I really do love it. I've always loved football. When other little girls were swooning over David Cassidy and Bobby Sherman, I was crushing on Bob Griese and Larry Csonka. OK, maybe I also had a little thing for David Cassidy…

At high school football games, while the other girls laughed and socialized in the stands, I would be yelling at the refs or trying to shout out plays from the bleachers. Post-high school, the football gods most definitely knew what they were doing when I ended up attending Florida State University, home of the FSU Seminoles — *GO*

NOLES! Don't even get me started on the legendary Bobby Bowden. BEST. COACH. EVER.

Most of my gal pals, including my mom, do not understand this transformation I undergo each fall. I do sometimes find it difficult to explain my all-out obsession with this sport. To be helpful, here are a few insights as to why each year I so look forward to the first weekend in September when the season kicks off anew:

Mondays, after all my teams have won. A perfect fall weekend for me is when all of my teams—the Seminoles, the Dolphins, the Nittany Lions (shout-out for Jimmy), and the Wolfpack (shout-out for husband Greg)—have won. There is of course an exception—when the Seminoles play the Wolfpack each year (they're both currently in the ACC), I am *all in* for FSU. Hubby understands this and steers clear.

A close game with little time left. There is nothing better than when a game comes down to the wire. The score is tied or separated by three or fewer points; the team with the ball is driving down the field; no time outs are left; the Hail Mary pass goes up. I swear I get a chill just thinking about it. How can you not?!

Armchair quarterbacking with my dad. I love to talk football with my dad. It's one of the best things we have in common, this love of the game. Every once in a while there's a little side wager. I'm pretty sure he's won a time or two more often than me, but I can hold my own, thank you very much.

The "Tomahawk Chop" and other traditions. It's an unforgettable experience to be perched in the stadium and feel the energy of 80,000 fans all moving and chanting in unison.

Whatever your tradition, you appreciate exactly what I mean when that buzz starts. I haven't been to a Florida State game in a while (never miss a televised game), but I will be attending one in October. I've got my Seminole fight song all ready to sing. I. CANNOT. WAIT. Lucky FSU sweatshirt circa 1984 is already packed.

See you in the bleachers. Oh, and one more thing…GO NOLES!!

Gardenias in Costco

WALKING THROUGH COSTCO, while pushing my oversized cart and desperately searching for the printer ink, I came across an aisle filled with gardenia bushes. The shrubs lined the aisle on both sides, blocking access to an array of bargain-priced household products. I stopped and took in the beautiful, dark green shiny leaves and emerging white buds, all of which made me think of my GeeGee.

In the backyard of the Florida home where I spent many of my childhood days, my grandmother, GeeGee, had the largest, most beautiful gardenia bush. She was such a good Southern gal who could grow anything. Tucked in among her orange and avocado trees and crotons was that bush.

As I stood there in aisle 14 of Costco, missing my GeeGee in the most aching way, I almost started bawling. Oh, yes, this new-found talent to go from stoic to Tammy Faye Baker in ten seconds or less is a nice little present from the menopause fairy. What stopped my impending blubbering, and caused me to instead let out a bit of a laugh, was GeeGee's voice chiming in, as if over the loud speaker,

"Oh, good Lord, such a fuss Kimberly, and in the middle of Costco! Bless your heart, it's just a plant."

God love that woman. She will always be my quintessential model of the classic Southern gal.

Southern women have been portrayed in a variety of ways throughout both literature and cinema. There is, of course, the mother of all Southern belles: Margaret Mitchell's Scarlett O'Hara of *Gone With the Wind* fame. Who could forget Tennessee Williams' Southern gal protagonists Blanche DuBois, or Maggie from *Cat On a Hot Tin Roof*? I have my personal favorites, including Susan Sarandon's wonderfully kooky Southern gal performance in *Bull Durham*.

Actress Sissy Spacek—a Southern gal herself as she hails from Quitman, Texas—noted in a recent interview that being Southern is a "state of mind." I believe this is most definitely true. The character of a Southern woman is not dependent upon her physical location but rather the way in which she perceives and carries herself each day—in fact, her state of mind.

The telltale Southern drawl can be the usual giveaway that a Southern girl is in the room. I don't personally possess much of a Southern twang, unless I'm tired or have perhaps consumed a wee too much tequila. Yet, I most definitely consider myself the product of a proper Southern upbringing, even without possessing much of an accent. What comes to mind for me, as examples of proper Southern gal traits and qualities I aspire to emulate and possess, include:

A certain sensibility. Southern gals possess an undeniable "matter-of-factness" about life. If the yard needs mowing, well then good gracious just go mow it! Even Scarlett O'Hara sucked it up and worked the fields when it was necessary.

Tomatoes. You gotta be able to grow 'maters. I'm still working on this one. To date I've let GeeGee down a bit here. I've mastered a modest, yet acceptable, sun garden, but 'maters have been my nemesis.

No swearing. Much to my own mother's dismay, this is an attribute I fail at—miserably and regularly. I can't seem to get through the day without a bevy of expletives escaping these Southern gal lips. In most circles this is not acceptable. I never once ever heard GeeGee utter anything rougher than "damn!" And God help you if that utterance was due to something you had said or done. Regarding swearing, if you do happen to ever hear a Southern gal utter the words "Ah... *HELL* no..." you better run.

An ability to maintain long-lasting gal pal relationships. GeeGee's ability to maintain lifelong friendships with her girlfriends and her sisters was something I learned to emulate at a young age. Two of my dearest friends have been by my side since I was fourteen years old. I would sincerely be lost without my gal pals. They hold me up most days.

No just running up to the store. GeeGee always looked "put together." Purse went with the shoes, dress complemented the purse, lipstick matched the nail polish. Even when she was working in the yard, I always remember her wearing a proper hat and gardening gloves. One of these days when I run up to the grocery store for only a few items, and I neglect to put on a clean shirt and a little mascara, this will be the day I run into George Clooney. When this happens I will surely hear GeeGee chuckling away.

A true heart. GeeGee certainly had strong convictions about most things. I didn't always agree with everything she said or did, but I admired her will. I never doubted she always believed she was doing the right thing for the right reason.

A little bit of mischief. Being a good Southern gal doesn't mean behaving like a saint. I imagine GeeGee got into her fair share of trouble throughout her life. During World War II she ran the United Services Organization (USO) in Jacksonville and I often picture her dancing and laughing with the sailors. Surely there was a little mischief to be had while jitterbugging with the boys.

Well, I gotta go. I need to head back to Costco. Can you believe I bought the gardenia bush, but forgot the printer ink? Dammit.

Three Little Words

THERE ARE PHRASES I'm quite sure I will never utter:

"Chocolate? No thanks."

"It's Free? Pass."

"Love the Gators." (OK, this one isn't even funny to joke about).

I did, however, recently find myself saying something I truly *never* thought I would ever pronounce:

"I miss Florida."

Even at a young age, I always had a plan to leave Florida just as soon as possible. BFF Dani has pointed out that I wrote in her high school yearbook, circa 1981, that I would be seeing her in DC, living in a row house in Georgetown, and working for the government. Well, I never made it to Georgetown, but the rest certainly held true.

I'm not sure why I was so hell bent on leaving the Sunshine State. Maybe it was merely one of those wanting-to-spread-your-wings/ leave-the-nest sorts of things. Dani and I have both recently admitted there are things we actually do miss about Florida. Is it nostalgic musings, or are the following observations legit?

By the way, you might notice Disney World is not featured on my top ten list: I'm not a Disney fan. Before I start getting swamped with all the hate mail, I recognize there is a cult of you out there who worship at the altar of all things Disney. Good for you. Your crazy love keeps Florida from ever having to create a state income tax. I'll spare everyone most of the details that rationalize my lukewarm feelings toward The Mouse. I will, however, leave you with this question: Why is it that in almost all (I say almost because I know, *I know*, there is at least one exception) of Disney's animated films Mom is dead or missing? Survey says: Hmm…

Top Ten Things I Miss About Florida

1. **I miss my family**. My mom, brother, uncles, and cousins all still live in Florida. I also have a large, extended network of friends who live there. I miss them all. I sometimes think about how nice it was to have my grandparents so close to me growing up and how I took for granted that I could easily walk to their house. There are days when I wish I could walk on over to Mom's for dinner.

2. **I miss the beach**. There is something downright soulful about the beach. The sand, the sound of the ocean, the simple act of lying on the beach and doing nothing. In my first book I have a story entitled "Flagpole" that describes what it was like to grow up near the beach. Each time I read that story I have an urge to go collect seashells.

3. **I miss access to a warm ocean**. I give this one its own ranking in the top ten. I was shocked to discover the ocean in coastal areas north of Florida is *cold*! You can't swim in that. It's not refreshing, it's an ice bath.

4. **I miss that the rain stops in less than one hour**. In Florida, the rain blows in—big, blustery, heavy tropical downpours—and then it's gone in about an hour. Your whole day does not get ruined by the weather. Today is a great example. Here in Virginia it's going to be gray and rainy and windy all day long. In Florida this mess would have cleared out by now.

5. **I miss Publix**. If you've never been to a Publix, you are missing out. Publix is the best grocery store food chain in the country. Alas, they are only located in the South, having gotten their start in Florida in 1930. Ya'll need to come farther north (just sayin').

6. **I miss fresh fruits and veggies all year round**. I absolutely took for granted that in Florida you have access to fresh produce any time of the year. The first time I ever tried to buy tomatoes in the winter in Virginia, I complained to the produce manager that they looked awful *and* were four dollars a pound. He looked at me and said, "You do know it's February, right?"

7. **I miss free tennis courts and public parks in every neighborhood**. The beach is free, and so are the many courts and parks in Florida. It makes for a wallet-friendly existence. If you're ever in FLA, I recommend you check out Jonathan Dickenson State Park or Dubois Park.

8. **I miss the lizards**. I bet this one seems a bit weird. However, the lizards are all over the place in Florida, and they're kind of cool.

9. **I miss tropical gardens**. I do love my peonies and my irises and my lilies, none of which will grow well in Florida. But, I miss tropical foliage too, like bougainvillea and crotons and big banyan trees.

10. **I miss Russo's**. Last, but certainly not least, I miss Russo's Subs. When Mom comes to Virginia for a visit, I beg her to bring Russo's with her. They are hands down the BEST. SUB. EVER. Don't believe, me? Check out their fan page on Facebook; a near-cult following if ever there was one.

Ain't No Place for Sissies

THIS PAST WEEKEND I attended a good friend's wedding—his second, her first. It was a beautiful and fun affair, a great way to start down the marital path. Not surprisingly, this event has had me reflecting a bit on marriages—first, second, and beyond.

I've been warned. *(Danger, Will Robinson, DANGER!)* Why would I ever want to wade into the minefield-laced topic of marriage? Well, kiddies, sometimes you just gotta get in there and throw out a few ideas. Let's be clear: I'm *not* a reliable expert on what makes a marriage work. I'm the antithesis of a marriage expert. In the dictionary, next to the phrase "marriage expert," you will *not* find my picture.

I do, of course, have a few observations regarding marriage. Kimba always has an opinion...

Marriage is hard. If you think you'll be happy every day, you're delusional. The great Bette Davis (one of my all-time favorite broads) was famous for saying, "Old age ain't no place for sissies." Her quote could easily be modified to read: "Marriage ain't for sissies, either."

I do think marriage is different the second time around. Yep, I'm happily on wedded bliss number two; been here going on fifteen years. For me, I'm simply a different person now. Older, wiser, and I don't sweat the small stuff nearly as much as I used to. It certainly helps that I continue to be invested in making my husband happy.

I'm not sure I was very good at this—recognizing and contributing to another person's happiness—the first time around.

One thing I am hopelessly bad at is compromise. And, if marriage is about anything, it's about compromise. I hate that I often fall into the stereotypical female mindset of "keeping score." I have to constantly try to wipe that slate clean. I actually should try to get rid of the slate all together.

It's easy to become jaded about the institution of marriage. I don't understand how women summon the courage to ever try matrimony more than once or twice. But, there are gals like the fabulous Elizabeth Taylor who never give up on nuptials. (I actually have an odd little connection to Ms. Taylor. In 1976, Taylor married husband number six, Senator John Warner, in a little church just outside of Leesburg, Virginia. Twenty-five years later, Greg and I exchanged vows in that same small, quaint country haven.)

Do I have any sound advice? Any little gems to pass along regarding the secrets of a happy marriage? Sorry, but no, I've got *nada*—no great personal insights to offer whatsoever.

I do recommend the sage wisdom of Jill Conner Browne, whose book *The Sweet Potato Queens' Book of Love* should be required reading for all newlyweds. Ms. Browne shares that for every woman, there are five men she must have in her life at all times:

1.   One you can talk to
2.   One who can fix things
3.   One you can dance with
4.   One who can pay for things
5.   One to have sex with

Newsflash: Numbers one through five above are not likely to all be the same guy, and that's perfectly OK. Your spouse should probably be number five. Also, I'm not personally vested in number four; I like to pay for my own stuff. However, numbers one through three are absolutely up for grabs. It's not realistic to think one person can cover all your needs all the time. Is it?

Stupid Sh*t Said to Women

A FRIEND RECENTLY suggested I read the interview of Hillary Clinton written by Cindi Leive, editor-in-chief of *Glamour* magazine. This September 2014 article focuses on career advice for women. The article was recommended because I've developed a keen interest in the whole "lean in versus be balanced" debate.

Clinton's discussion of what it was like to be a woman taking the law school admissions test back in the early seventies is particularly thought-provoking. She recalls men saying to her:

"What are you doing here?"

"You shouldn't be here."

"You're taking the place of a man who could maybe get drafted and die in Vietnam."

Fast forward to today when the percentage of women in law school is hovering around forty-six percent. Overall, we may not be equal, but we've certainly progressed past overt discrimination... right? I've been wondering:

Have we come a long way, baby?

As if on cue, this past week I was quickly reminded that there continue to be boneheads out there who say the dumbest sh*t ever to and about women. Fox News "The Five" host Eric Bolling, reporting about airstrikes against Syria, asked if the United Arab Emirates' first female fighter pilot, Major Mariam al-Mansouri, amounted to *boobs on the ground*.

Oh, but that's not all! While you watch, make note that his cohort in stupidity, a broadcaster named Greg Gutfeld, also quipped: "Problem is, after she bombed [with] it, she couldn't park it."

Welcome to 2014, where we're still dealing with this kind of flat-out sexist ridicule. To ensure it's not just me who is getting tired of this sort of BS, I sent a little query to my gal pal peeps, asking them their experiences with remarks that would never be said to, or about, men. Wow, did I get an earful! Special thanks to the women over on *Midlife Boulevard* who provided so much material I may very well have the beginnings of a new book.

Stupid Sh*t Said to Women (but never to men)

You're not one of those feminists, are you?

You look great for your age.

You seem a little upset. Is it, you know, cycle-related?

It's a man's world. (WTF does that even *mean*?!)

My husband would never let me cut my hair that short.

Or...

Are you growing your hair out?

Or...

What does your husband think of your haircut? (I can guarantee you, no one has ever asked the Hubs what I think of his 'do.)

At work, while pregnant with her fourth child, a friend was asked, "What kind of birth control do you use?"

Perhaps I should speak with your husband. (Or,) Don't you need to ask your husband?

You sure know a lot about football, for a girl. (Anything followed by *for a girl*, is officially stupid.)

Would you mind taking notes... getting coffee... (or) cleaning off the conference table?

Well, you're just big-boned.

Cute outfit, did you borrow in from your daughter? Your mother? (Can you imagine anyone *ever* asking a guy if he borrowed a jacket from his son?)

Combating this stupidity, calling it out when it happens, takes time, patience, and the occasional use of one's middle finger. I'm most definitely up for the challenge. Have face palm, will travel.

Verbal Cues and Vocal Frys: Oh Muh Gawd!

ONE OF MY FAVORITE THINGS to do on a Sunday morning is spread out the Washington Post on the coffee table, settle in with a good cup of joe, and watch *CBS Sunday Morning*. During a recent broadcast they discussed a relatively new phenomenon known as "The Vocal Fry."* Being that French fries are my all-time favorite junk food, my interest was immediately piqued.

Turned out to not be exactly what I had been expecting.

It's a little difficult to explain a vocal fry. It's a guttural tapering off at the end of a sentence that conveys condescension, a kind of world-weariness, or—to me—stupidity. Think Kim Kardashian (ugh, I hate to even mention her). This entire generation of young women seems to be just so bored with it all.

As I was later lamenting about these disaffected women of today—honestly, what's their problem?!—I got called on it. Pot to kettle: Guess what? You're black.

Here's the thing, I grew up in the time of valley speak. OH MUH GAWD! was the mantra of the day. I would've surely been offended if all women of the eighties, including me, were categorized as Valley Girls. But in the interest of full disclosure, I did use the terms "like" and "for sure" way too often. Still do. It's been suggested that perhaps I shouldn't be so quick to judge the vocal fry gals.

All this talk about verbal communications has me also thinking about my own verbal cues; little personal ticks or traits I use to communicate during discussions. For example, one of my verbal cues that drives my dad nuts is during a conversation, when I agree with you, I'll emphatically reply,

"Exactly!"

Then I lean in and proceed to explain why I believe you're right. It's a way to interrupt and insert my own opinion. Yes, it's a bit obnoxious.

I also have a shortcut I use to disagree with someone. If you say something I don't necessarily agree with, I will utter a fairly dismissive,

"Huh."

That's it. Talk about a conversation killer. In one little three-letter word I've shot you down.

In my current heightened state of verbal awareness, I've also noticed the cues of others. For example, one of my best gal pals uses a cue that is non-verbal, but quite effective. When she disagrees with something being said, she presses her lips together and raises her eyebrows, to seemingly convey, *I really don't agree with you, but I'm too nice to say it out loud, so I'll suppress my displeasure, but I want you to know I think you're wrong.* According to the Center for Non-Verbal Studies this is known as "lip compression."

My mom's verbal cues are my favorites. When we are in the car, if she doesn't like the way I'm driving, she will occasionally pronounce,

"Ewwwww!"

I cannot do justice to the affect this sound has on me. In one utterance she's able to convey that the driver needs to slow down, move over, put on the turn signal, wait for the car to pass, and turn left.

I guess in the end we all have to find our voice. Valley speak or vocal fry, we all learn to convey our feelings. So perhaps I shouldn't be so quick to judge these younger women who are working diligently to effectively communicate, right?

Huh.

www.cbsnews.com/news/faith-salie-burned-out-on-the-fry/

Why Women are ALWAYS Late

A GUY FRIEND (not Hubs) recently lamented: Why are women *always* late?

Oh, this is an easy one. I got this.

When a man leaves the house each morning:

1. The TV is on—in every room.

2. Yesterday's clothes are on the floor.

3. Dirty dishes are in the sink.

4. The kitty litter box is overflowing.

5. The kids are still in bed.

6. Though he probably takes a shower, the shaving is optional.

7. He grabs the first pair of pants in the closet that aren't on the floor.

8. He will make a pit stop at McDonalds for breakfast.

When a woman leaves the house each morning:

1. The dog has been walked, fed, and groomed.

2. All electronics are off and unplugged.

3. Tonight's dinner is in the crock pot.

4. The laundry is done, folded, and put away.

5. The kitchen is spotless, sanitized and fresh flowers are on the counter.

6. She's showered, shaved her legs, washed, blow-dried and styled her hair, put on make-up and gone through five outfits before she's decided what to wear.

7. The kids are up, dressed, fed, had their backpacks checked (twice), and are out the door to wait for the school bus. By the way, Mom doesn't leave the neighborhood until she sees the bus drive by.

8. She's made a protein smoothie to take with her on the commute.

There you have it, this is why women are always late. Any questions?

Response from guy friend: "Can I buy the next round?"

Why, yes. Yes, you can.

My Middle-Aged Bucket

ONE DOES NOT THINK too much about bucket lists when one is young. You're too busy rushing forward to be concerned about the things you're not doing. During my first five decades I was full steam ahead, go-go-go, to-do list in hand busily checking off items and then quickly moving on to the next adventure. Hey, I'm a Virgo, of course I had a to-do list—don't judge.

Something started changing the closer I got to Club Fifty status. There's been a small yet perceivable shift in perspective. I've found myself asking this question quite a bit lately: "To where am I sprinting?" Hmm...

In celebration of my upcoming fifty-first birthday, and to remind myself to slow down—change the sprint to a stroll—I've put some thought into how I'd like to fill my bucket. I've come up with fifty-one goals I'd like to accomplish before I leave this world. Some of these ambitions are tangible and specific, others are a bit more philosophical. All represent this crazy Southern Irish gal's glance back over her shoulder for a little inspiration.

In no particular order, I would like to:

1. Master the art of a decent pie crust. This one is kinda embarrassing. As a good Southern gal I should have this locked up.

2. Grow my hair out one more time.

3. Hold my grandchild. (No pressure Jimmy, none whatsoever…)

4. Be published by Huffington Post. I think *this* post would work nicely, don't you? HuffPost50, HuffPostWomen— anyone, anyone?

5. Splash in a fountain in Italy.

6. Meet a U.S. President. #nerdalert.

7. Sit in the gallery during a State of the Union address. #supernerdalert.

8. Talk less/listen more.

9. Host a party for my high school buddies, but not a "reunion." A good ol' fashioned throwdown. TLHS Class of 1981, you in?

10. Learn to play golf. I've got the left-handed clubs all ready to go.

11. Score tickets to a Prince concert. Must figure out how to get backstage this time.

12. Meet George Clooney. (Full disclosure: This one has been in the bucket a long time.)

13. Visit my family more often.

14. Dedicate some significant time to yoga.

15. Finish my genealogy research. I currently have a full list of my great-great grandparents, and I can follow some lineage back

to the 1500s. But I would like to dig deep to discover more family stories.

16. Find hidden treasures along the "World's Longest Yard Sale." Occurs first week of August each year. Would very much like to do this with my dad. (www.127sale.com/)

17. Sip real French Champagne—in France.

18. Grow decent 'maters. I'm on the verge of having my good Southern girl card revoked if I don't give number 18 some sincere attention.

19. Appreciate the Hubs more—Thanks, Hon.

20. Attend an auction. Any kind of auction. Well, except a live-stock auction. I don't need to acquire cattle.

21. Learn to use a power saw. I know, tempting fate here.

22. Volunteer more. Mom and Jimmy, you're my inspiration for this one.

23. Be a seat filler at the Academy Awards. This is not an urban myth: www.seeing-stars.com/ShowBiz/SeatFillers.shtml

24. Honor my size 11 feet. They make me, me. Left-handed, green-eyed—it's all good.

25. Learn all the words to "Hook" by Blues Traveler.

26. Make the perfect margarita. I may be close on this one. Practice, practice, practice.

27. Converse in sign language.

28. Publish *Magic Fishing Panties*. Hello, publishers? Call me. 1-800-havefulldraft. (Newsflash: If you're reading this now, we can check this off!)

29. Not be such a Virgo/make peace with being a Virgo.

30. Promote #embracethecougar as a national movement.

31. Remember that when in doubt, give 'em the benefit of the doubt.

32. See the Aurora Borealis.

33. Be kinder. Everyone carries a bag of rocks.

34. Give up the quest to understand men. They are truly a completely different species. Don't think so? I give you Exhibit A: farting.

35. Laugh at all the wrong parts of a movie. Oh, wait, I can definitely mark this one off my list.

36. Write one great, memorable line of dialogue.

37. Get *serious* about flossing.

38. Be unpredictable.

39. Build a sandcastle with a five-year-old.

40. Appreciate life.

41. Learn to drive stick.

42. Beat Hobbit at *Words With Friends*. Oh, *you* know.

43. Find the perfect mascara and buy cases of it so when it's discontinued I'm not left high and dry.

44. Visit Niagara Falls, Canadian side. Bonus: stay in the kitschiest honeymoon suite possible. Heart-shaped bed kind of kitschy.

45. Leave behind enough material to inspire someone to write a kick-ass epitaph.

46. Start a national dialogue about "life on the balance beam." Maybe women don't want to "lean in" and be the boss; maybe what we want is to be happy and have a balanced life. Sorry, Sheryl.

47. Write in wet cement.

48. Have good reason to throw a drink in someone's face. Or, perhaps have a drink thrown in my face, for good reason. It just seems so dramatic!

49. Learn to read tarot cards.

50. Do an unassisted pull-up.

51. Leave room for a little mystery.

I've shown you mine, now you show me yours—what's in your bucket?

Club Fifty

ACCORDING TO THE Centers for Disease Control and Prevention, there are more than four million of us in the United States who claim 1963 as the year of our birth. We barely squeaked into the baby boomer generation, which includes those born between 1946 and 1964. Our sub-group (and many millions more world-wide) collectively joined Club Fifty in 2013, finishing our fifth decade here and realizing the not-so-shocking reality that we are now officially the older generation.

A quick factoid: A person aged fifty years, or in their fifties, is known as a *quinquagenarian*. Am I the only one who has a difficult time pronouncing quin·qua·ge·nar·i·an?

The one event that most recount almost immediately when recalling 1963 is that President Kennedy was tragically assassinated in Dallas, Texas, in November of that year. I got to thinking: what else—events, people—celebrated admission to Club Fifty along with me in 2013? For whom else was 2013 a significant milestone?

* Two televisions shows I definitely remember from my child-hood debuted in 1963: *My Favorite Martian* and *The French Chef* (hosted by Julia Child). MFM in particular exemplifies

the campiness of many of the sitcoms from the sixties. Were you a fan?

* 2013 was the fiftieth anniversary of the release of The Beatles' first album, *Please Please Me*, which burst onto the music scene on March 22, 1963. This album (yes, they were called *albums* back in 1963) also included *I Saw Her Standing There* and *Love Me Do*. You're welcome for that little earworm.

* *Amazing Spider-Man #1* hit shelves on March 10, 1963. If you happened to be around in 1963 and purchased this little comic for twelve cents, you are now the proud owner of a collectible worth an estimated $40,000.

* I appear to be in good company. Others who marked Club Fifty status in 2013 included Johnny Depp, Michael Jordan, Brad Pitt, and Jennifer Beals—I still love the tunes from her iconic 1980s film, *Flashdance*.

* Celebrating with me were the members of the Twin Lakes High School Class of 1981—almost all joined *Club Fifty* last year. I hope you all had very happy birthdays and GO RAMS (been quite a while since I exclaimed those two words).

I've experienced quite a few life lessons over these past five decades. Club admission brings with it a laundry list of experiences, both good and bad, which become our platform for touting age and experience over youth and exuberance. These lessons can emerge at the most interesting of moments. Take, for example, this recent interchange with my husband, Greg. Here's how it went down:

I'd been pestering the Hubs to start laying out on the dresser his clothes, and his everyday must-haves, for the next day before he climbed into bed each night. He's a grown man, and he can certainly dress himself, but I had become weary of the in-the-dark hunt around the bedroom in search of matching socks, shoes, cell phone, car keys, belt, etc. He had obliged and it had been working out pretty well, until…

One early morning, all snuggled up under the covers, I groggily awakened to the sounds of Hubby grumbling and bumping around the bedroom. I soon realized he was muttering,

"Dammit, where is it… I know I laid it out with my clothes…"

He was clearly on the hunt for something.

"Honey, what are you looking for?" I mumbled.

"My undershirt," he replied. "How can an undershirt get up and walk away?"

Lying there, under the covers, it slowly occurred to me: I was wearing his undershirt. I had stayed up late the night before, watching Jimmy Fallon, and had quickly grabbed the shirt off the dresser and donned it before I jumped into bed. BUSTED! Did I 'fess up? Oh, hell no.

"Well, just get another one out of the bureau," said the gal lying there in the comfy white cotton undershirt with the quilt pulled up to her chin.

"Fine, I'm really trying to make a peaceful exit outta here in the mornings. Sorry."

He said sorry… to me.

Because I'm a big believer in karma and the universal righting of wrongs, I did come clean as soon as he walked in the door that night and I apologized… a lot. He thought it was funny. Yep, have I told you how cool my husband is?

I had another occasion where a little fib taught me a good life lesson about how even small lies can come back to bite you in the butt. Well, it wasn't exactly a lie, it was more like an ongoing sight gag. Back in my early forties I used to joke: "Hey, don't I look great… for *fifty*?" I said this so often it became a running joke.

Until…

When I turned forty-nine I made a comment about having one more year before I joined *Club Fifty*. My brother-in-law replied,

"Wait a minute. I've heard you make jokes about looking great for fifty for a while… what do you mean you're *not yet fifty*?"

OUCH!!! Funny, but, really?! Have I now put myself in the position to have to change my tune to: "Don't I look great… for *sixty*?" Well I got no one to blame but the gal in the mirror for this one.

Is it ever OK to tell a little white lie? I do have a few personal rules about this subject. These I've added to my Club Fifty lessons-learned playbook:

It is *always ok* to lie about babies. There was a great Seinfeld episode (honestly, weren't they all great?) where the gang was stressing about attending a bris where the baby was portrayed as less than beautiful. OK, *all* babies are beautiful, but, I can see where from time to time you might come across a little one who may not be your ideal of beauty. *Do not be honest here.* If all else fails, go with: "That's a fine baby." This is the equivalent of *bless your heart* in the South; kind of a linguistic get-out-of-jail-free card.

It's OK to lie about your weight… or your height. All women want to weigh 125 pounds and all men want to be six feet tall. So be it. Some will argue that by the time we achieve Club Fifty status we should have learned to be happy with who we are, no matter our weight or height. Well, good for you. For the rest of us, yes, I weigh 125 pounds.

It's OK to tell a little fib about how much you paid for a cute skirt or pair of must-have pumps. However, be warned: Don't ever ask me how much I paid for a dress. My mama taught me that asking how much something costs is rude. I get that this might just be a Southern thing. My go-to response to this question, which is not a lie, is: "It cost enough." If you feel the need to lie a little here, go ahead. You have my permission.

It's almost never OK to lie to your spouse, especially about money, sex, or kids. If anyone can give me a good reason to alter this rule, I'm all ears.

Here's to the joys of Club Fifty membership and all the wisdom it brings. A belated happy birthday to all my fellow members who share the 1963 birth year. We should have all received our AARP cards by now. Who wants to meet me at the Denny's down the street for the senior breakfast?

Kimba's Tip of the Day

I'M NOT A BIG FAN of unsolicited advice. My propensity to spout off has often gotten me into trouble and pissed off my friends and family who get sick of my know-it-all tendencies. I work diligently to quiet the girl in my head who has a running dialogue in every conversation about how she can fix a particular problem or opine about any current political issue. If I could only adhere to some of the best advice my mama ever gave me: *Opinions are like belly buttons—everybody has one, doesn't mean you always have to share it with the world.*

Luckily, I've found an outlet: the Internet.

I've taken to putting out there, on a regular basis, what has come to be termed "Kimba's Tip of the Day." One of my gal pals coined this phrase, and it stuck. Sometimes it's a post on Facebook, sometimes it's just a little random tweet. It's a win-win: I can put my opinions, thoughts, and observations out there for all the world to see, and the minions can ignore me without hurting my feelings one little bit.

In case you've had trouble keeping up, presented below are some of my favorites. A few need a bit of explanation, others I'll leave to your imagination.

Snakes are never a laughing matter:

Kimba: I need you to come with me right now.
Starbucks employee: Why, ma'am? What's wrong?
Kimba: Um, there's a snake is the ladies room.
#ishityounot #thingsyoudontheareveryday

*   *   *

You can never review your credit history enough:

What type of credit card thief tries to charge $1,200 at diapers.com?!
They vastly underestimated my husband and his genius detective
skillz. #gratefulwife

*   *   *

No woman ever started an argument with a man while he was
dusting, vacuuming, or washing the dishes. (Not original, but a
valuable tip worth repeating.)

*   *   *

Don't jump the gun:

Just received an e-mail for "local singles over 50 looking for love."
First of all, I ain't single. Second, I ain't 50 for another 14 days!
Jump the gun much?! #WTF #amiright

*   *   *

Sometimes it's better to simply smile and walk away:

That moment when the male employee is walking out of the ladies
room and hurriedly explains he was "just cleaning." #awkward
#methinkshedothprotesttoomuch

* * *

Your hair is a completely unpredictable animal:

Having a good hair day—completely wasted on the only signifi-cant item on today's to-do list being the annual mammogram. #hairgoddesslaughing

Some mornings your only option is to wear a hat. #badhairday

* * *

Having car-related issues has been an ongoing theme:

If you're going to own a silver car, you gotta come up with a system for remembering where you parked. #newcarproblems #popularcar-colors #101waystofindyourcar

It's a waste of time to walk around the parking lot looking for your Jeep, if your Jeep is in the shop and you're driving a rental. #justsayin

All Thrifty had for car rental (because my flight was late getting in) was a Crown Vic. Everyone around me will be driving the speed limit.

* * *

If the Sephora sales girl hadn't gone straight to the "I know the perfect anti-aging cream for you," she would have made a bigger sale. I get the whole "read your customer" thing, but couldn't she have also thrown a little mascara a gal's way? #middleagedproblems

* * *

Grocery shopping when you're hungry is such a good idea... Said no one, ever. Doritos is a healthy food group, right?

* * *

A girl should NEVER attend a party with hairy knees. #justsayin

* * *

Girlfriends do not let girlfriends wear horizontal stripes. #justsayin

* * *

If you're going to be smug, be naked smug:

Greg is having to endure my Democrat happy dance today. To be fair, I did do it naked. #ohnoshedidnt #goodday2Bblue

* * *

Reality bites:

Scene: Atlanta airport, chatting up James Marsden's doppelganger.
Him: So, what do you do?
Me: I'm a writer.
Him: Cool, do you have a book out?
Me: Why, yes, yes I do. Here's a bookmark.
Him (taking bookmark and laughing): Great title. My *mom* will love this.
(Cue hubby laughing and spitting up margarita.)
He couldn't have said sister...Or even girlfriend?
#middleagedflirtingproblems

* * *

Middle-schoolers suck:

While walking Taz this morning, he decided to "do his business" right next to the school bus that was loading. The kids applauded and started chanting 'PICK UP THE POOP! PICK UP THE POOP!' Really... at 7 a.m.? #middleschoolerssuck

*   *   *

Don't mess with middle-aged women and their work-outs:

Dear twenty-somethings who have invaded the weight-training class: It's not acceptable to work out in a sports bra and no shirt. The middle-agers are plotting countermeasures. This will be your only warning.

*   *   *

Need writing inspiration? Head to Costco:

Mom, can we get the Spider-Man undies? (Yes, I let the Hubs buy the twelve pack...)

*   *   *

Asking husbands for fashion advice is truly a waste of time:

Me: Honey, which of these four pairs of shoes goes best with this dress?
Greg: The black ones.
They were all black.

*   *   *

God love the cheesy pick-up line:

Bless the man at the deli counter who asked me if I was buying lunchmeat to get ready to send my kids back to school. I don't care if it was a cheesy line, bless him.

*   *   *

Leaving a dirty dish in the sink will make most women go bat-crap crazy. #amiwrong

*   *   *

Menopause sucks:

Put on glasses and check in the mirror because DAMN when did I become the bearded lady?!

*   *   *

Rules to live by:

Hey! Only two rules to live by: There's no crying in baseball and no calling dibs on Mr. Clooney!

*   *   *

If your shoes stick to the bar floor, you may want to rethink using the bar bathroom. #justsayin

*   *   *

Few joys compare to finding the lost bottle of Afrin when you have a head cold. #justsayin

*   *   *

Here's a dieting tip anyone can use:

Doritos Locos Tacos—crazy good and only 170 calories. Who knew? BEST. NEWS. EVER.

*   *   *

Two hours to clear paper jam = it would have been easier to address the envelope by hand.

*   *   *

As important as picking a perfect mate, a gal must find a perfect drycleaner, hairstylist and gyno.

*   *   *

Never underestimate the appeal of a man who can handle a shovel:

Getting up at 5:30 a.m. to shovel driveway and take me to the metro = best husband of the day award. #thankshoney

*   *   *

There is something about seeing a woman driving with curlers in her hair that just makes me grin. #randomuselessstuff

*   *   *

Fact: I will watch any of the 'Rush Hour' movies just to see the outtakes at the end.

*   *   *

It's just the way the universe works:

Sixteen rows of condoms, but it takes a team of sales associates to locate a box of Band-aids. Welcome to shopping in a college town. #justsayin

* * *

There are places in southern Virginia where you can buy oysters, get your taxes done, and have your propane tank filled—all at the same time. #goodtoknow

* * *

To the woman who was "cock-blocking" me at Starbucks: Haha, I got my order first! And I wished her a good day. #itsthelittlethings #karmaisabitch

* * *

FACT: If you're in a hurry and running in for only a few things, you will: grab the most deformed cart—the Quasimodo of shopping carts—drop the eggs, and get stuck behind the woman in the checkout line who is challenging the cashier because the 40-cents-off Tide coupon did not show up on her receipt. #mamasaidtheredbedayslikethese

* * *

A sincere thank you to Al Gore (he did invent the Internet, right?), Jack Dorsey, and Mark Zuckerberg. Your innovations have saved many of my relationships by providing an outlet for my musings, thoughts, opinions, and occasional rants. This crazy Southern Irish gal is eternally in your debt.

Acknowledgments

I could never have imagined when my first essay was published that I would find myself five years later thanking everyone who has encouraged and supported this crazy addiction that is my writing. By the grace of all the funny and outrageous women who have come before us, we've somehow managed to birth another book. First and foremost, my undying gratitude goes to Booktrope Publishing which miraculously agreed to a partnership. God bless you—I would offer up my first born but he's in graduate school right now and I can't use him to repay my debts until about 2018. Thanks go to my editor, Anaik Alcasas, who tirelessly tweaked all my idiosyncrasies until they resembled something close to readable material. Much thanks also is due my book manager April Gerard, whose job title should include keeper of sanity, cheerleader, coach, and soul saver. I am forever beholden to the crazy talented Lizzie Russell, my book designer, who somehow reached into her magical design bag and created the perfect cover. Last but not least, thanks go to my proofreader and gal pal for life, Andie Gibson. I'm eternally grateful for everything this gifted woman has done for me with this book and beyond.

I am truly lucky to have found a home within the Virginia Writers Club, in particular the wonderful subchapter known as the Lake

Writers. I will forever be indebted to Andie Gibson (yep, again!), the former editor of *Smith Mountain Laker Magazine,* who took a gamble by offering me the humor column that is now *Dock Tale Hour*.

None of this—*nada*—would have ever been possible without the hand-holding and oftentimes late-night tequila shot consumption provided by Bets, Dani, Monkee, Kathi, Jane, Jill, and Barbara. You are all gal pals extraordinaire.

Every day I am thankful for the wonderful online sisterhood that encourages me to write fearlessly, live life out loud, and laugh often. The online communities at *The Women of Facebook, The Women of Midlife* (Sharon and Anne*), Better After 50 Writers* (Ronna), *Very Funny Women,* and *Humor Writers of America*, provided safe haven when I was very unsteady in my size 11 boots (and continue to do so today). Writers such as Vikki Claflin, Elaine Ambrose, Kate Mayer, Marcia Kester Doyle, Astra Groskaufmanis, Amy Sherman, Marquita Herald, and Gina Barreca have inspired me in ways they cannot possibly fully comprehend. Finally, to everyone in the Erma Bombeck Writers' Workshop Class of 2014, I can't wait to raise a cocktail with you in 2016.

Book Club Discussion Questions

1. Did you enjoy the book? Which story was your favorite? Why? Which story did you find funniest?

2. What was unique about the book settings and how did they enhance or take away from any of the stories? For example, to appreciate a story based in DC, do you feel you need to have lived in the DC area?

3. What themes did the author emphasize throughout the book? What do you think she was trying to convey to the reader?

4. Do the individuals portrayed in the book seem real and believable? Can you relate to their predicaments? To what extent do they remind you of yourself or someone you know?

5. In what ways do the events in the book reveal evidence of the author's world/life view?

6. Did certain parts of the book make you uncomfortable? If so, why did you feel that way? Did this lead to a new understanding

or awareness of some aspect of your life you might not have thought about before?

7.   The author tends to get herself into more than one embarrassing situation. What's the most embarrassing thing that's happened to you that you'd be willing to share with others?

8.   The book is written from the perspective of a woman over age 50. Do you think that only women over 50 will enjoy/understand this book, or would others appreciate it, too? Why or why not?

9.   Have you ever done anything you later regretted (such as getting a tattoo)?

10. Would you recommend this book to other readers? To your close friend? Why or why not?

Book Club Recommended Playlist

1. *We're Gonna Go Fishin'*, Hank Locklin
2. *I'm Walking on Sunshine*, Katrina and the Waves
3. *Cougar,* 2 Live Crew
4. *We Are Family*, Sister Sledge
5. *Leaving on a Jet Plane*, John Denver
6. *Tattoo*, Hunter Hayes
7. *Girls Just Wanna Have Fun*, Cyndi Lauper
8. *Florida State Fight Song,* Florida State University Marching Band
9. *When Irish Eyes Are Smiling*, The Irish Tenors
10. *Let's Go Crazy*, Prince
11. *Southern Nights*, Glen Campbell
12. *I'm Every Woman*, Whitney Houston
13. *Express Yourself*, Madonna
14. *Very Superstitious*, Stevie Wonder
15. *All I Want to Do Is Have Some Fun*, Sheryl Crow
16. *Stronger (What Doesn't Kill You)*, Kelly Clarkson
17. *Romeo*, Dolly Parton
18. *You're My Best Friend*, Queen
19. *So What*, P!nk
20. *Thank You For Being a Friend*, Andrew Gold

Additional Works by Kimberly J. Dalferes

I Was In Love With a Short Man Once (2015, 2011)

Nekkid Came the Swimmer (contributing writer, 2015)

Virginia Writers Club, Inc. Virtual Anthology (2015)

Virginia Writers Club, Inc. Virtual Anthology (2014)

Dock Tale Hour (humor column,
Smith Mountain Laker Magazine, since 2014)

Voices from Smith Mountain Lake (Anthology, 2013)

Author's Bio

Kimberly "Kimba" Dalferes is a native Floridian who currently pretends to be a Virginian. She is an accomplished king salmon slayer, estate sale junkie, and sometimes writes books. Her first book, *I Was In Love With a Short Man Once*, was published in 2011.

Dalferes' stories have been featured in diverse publications, including *Voices from Smith Mountain Lake* (an anthology published in 2013 by the Smith Mountain Arts Council), *The Roanoke Times*, *Hippocampus Magazine*, *Marco Polo Arts Magazine*, *The Business of Being an Author*, *Better After 50*, *Laugh Lines: Finding Your Funny*, *Erma Bombeck Writers' Workshop*, and *Midlife Boulevard*. Her humor column, *Dock Tale Hour*, appears in each issue of the bimonthly *Smith Mountain Laker Magazine*. She recently had a limerick published in *The Washington Post*, which she emphatically claims as a legitimate publication cred.

The author happily serves on the Board of Governors for the Virginia Writers Club (VWC), is a member of the Orangeberry Book Tours Hall of Fame (2012), and is a featured writer in *The Authors Show, 50 Great Writers You Should Be Reading* (2012). She won gold in the AUTHORSdb 2013 Book Cover Contest and has been recognized for her nonfiction writing as winner of the 2014 *Golden Nib Award*, VWC's highest honor.

Dalferes divides her time between Fairfax and Smith Mountain Lake, Virginia, with husband Greg, Bonz the cat, and occasionally son Jimmy, when he is home from college. She also can be found on a regular basis hanging out in *The Middle-Aged Cheap Seats*—her blog. She continues to sing hopelessly off key and waits patiently for that phone call from George Clooney.

Photo: Melissa Winn Photography

Don't forget to visit

www.kimdalferes.com

for author news, story excerpts, contests, humor blog posts and much more.

* * *

Connect with Kimba on social media, too!

Facebook.com/KimDalferes

@kimdalferes on Twitter

The Middle-Aged Cheap Seats (blog)

+KimDalferes on Google+

Kimdalferes on Pinterest

MORE GREAT READS
FROM BOOKTROPE

A Walk in the Snark by **Rachel Thompson** (Humor / Essays) Snark: It's not all humor, but it is all real. Humor and real life, with a little satire thrown in. Can you handle the snark?

The Mancode: Exposed by **Rachel Thompson** (Humor / Essays) Looking for a humorous take on family relationships, or love and romance? Look no further! Thompson deconstructs relationships with a keen, satirical eye in this humorous, #1 best selling essay collection.

Three-Year-Olds Are A**holes by **Sarah Fader** (Humor) Three-year-old Samantha is determined to make a rainbow, no matter the cost to her mother's sanity. A story of love and frustration.

American Goulash by **Stephanie Yuhas** (Memoir / Humor) A story about a nerd girl jousting with her Transylvanian family on the battlefields of suburban New Jersey for a chance to grow up authentically awkward and live a so-called normal American life.

Bumbling into Body Hair – A Transsexual's Memoir by **Everett Maroon** (Memoir) A comical memoir about a klutz's sex change, showing how a sense of humor—and true love—can triumph over hair disasters, and even the most crippling self-doubt.

Discover more books and learn about our
new approach to publishing at **www.booktrope.com**.